THE SOVIET DEFENCE INDUSTRY

D1565662

THE SOVIET DEFENCE INDUSTRY
CONVERSION AND ECONOMIC REFORM

Julian Cooper

PUBLISHED IN NORTH AMERICA FOR

THE ROYAL INSTITUTE OF INTERNATIONAL AFFAIRS

COUNCIL ON FOREIGN RELATIONS PRESS
• NEW YORK •

Chatham House Papers

A Soviet Programme Publication
Programme Director: Neil Malcolm

The Royal Institute of International Affairs, at Chatham House in London, has provided an impartial forum for discussion and debate on current international issues for 70 years. Its resident research fellows, specialized information resources, and range of publications, conferences, and meetings span the fields of international politics, economics, and security. The Institute is independent of government.

Chatham House Papers are short monographs on current policy problems which have been commissioned by the RIIA. In preparing the papers, authors are advised by a study group of experts convened by the RIIA, and publication of a paper indicates that the Institute regards it as an authoritative contribution to the public debate. The Institute does not, however, hold opinions of its own; the views expressed in this publication are the responsibility of the author.

Library of Congress Cataloguing-in-Publication Data

Cooper, Julian, 1945–
    The Soviet defence industry : conversion and economic reform / Julian Cooper.
         p.   cm. -- (Chatham House papers)
    "A Soviet Foreign Policy Programme publication."
    Includes bibliographical references.
    ISBN 0-87609-117-6 : $14.95
    1. Defence industries--Soviet Union. 2. Economic conversion--Soviet Union. I. Title. II. Series: Chatham House papers (Unnumbered)
HD9743.S672C66   1991
338.4'76233'0947--dc20

                        91-39922
                        CIP

91 92 93 94 95 96 97 PB 10 9 8 7 6 5 4 3 2 1

CONTENTS

ACKNOWLEDGMENTS

This paper is the outcome of research into the Soviet defence industry undertaken over several years. It owes much to discussion and contact with many colleagues, too numerous to mention, in Britain, Western Europe, the United States and the Soviet Union. The encouragement and assistance of colleagues at the University of Birmingham is gratefully acknowledged. Jackie Johnson, the former librarian of the Baykov Library, and Hugh Jenkins, the information officer of the Centre for Russian and East European Studies, facilitated access to valuable source material; Dr Michael Bradshaw of the School of Geography introduced me to the marvels of computer mapping. I am especially grateful to Neil Malcolm, the Director of the Soviet Programme at the Royal Institute of International Affairs, for inviting me to write this paper, and for his friendly but firm encouragement to meet seemingly impossible deadlines. I also wish to thank the members of the RIIA study group which discussed a draft of the paper for their many helpful criticisms and suggestions. The skilful editorial work of Hannah Doe of the RIIA has also been much appreciated.

The experience of writing this volume illustrates well the folly of attempting to capture the fast-changing reality of Soviet life in book form. The manuscript was almost ready for the printer when eight disgruntled, but inept, adventurers tried to seize power. In the week following the failed coup, some essential revisions were made, but I am keenly aware that by the time of publication more will be required.

The completion of this book would have been difficult, if not impossible, without the support of Silvana, so distant but always close. I dedicate it to her in gratitude.

September 1991   Julian Cooper

GLOSSARY AND ABBREVIATIONS

MIC: military-industrial complex
Minatomenergoprom: Ministry for Atomic Power and Industry
Minaviaprom: Ministry of the Aviation Industry
Minelektronprom: Ministry of the Electronics Industry
Minoboronprom: Ministry of the Defence Industry
Minobshchemash: Ministry of General Machinebuilding
Minradprom: Ministry of the Radio Industry
Minsredmash: Ministry of Medium Machinebuilding
Minsudprom: Ministry of the Shipbuilding Industry
Minsvyaz': Ministry of Communications
NPO (nauchno-proizvodstvennoe ob"edinenie): science-production association
Oblast': region or province – an administrative subdivision within a republic
PO (proizvodstvennoe ob"edinenie): production association
VPK: Military-Industrial Commission

THE SOVIET DEFENCE INDUSTRY

1
INTRODUCTION

The Soviet defence industry, the privileged heart of the state-dominated economy, is now in turmoil. As the country moves towards a market economy, the Soviet 'military-industrial complex' (MIC) is attempting to adapt to defence budget cuts, partial conversion to civil purposes and the unaccustomed conditions of glasnost. As republics, cities and regions assert their autonomy, the defence industry, like its civilian counterpart, is experiencing growing economic dislocation. Whereas in the past its employees were a well-paid and honoured elite, they now face loss of status, insecurity and hostility from sections of the public convinced that a hypertrophied military effort bears prime responsibility for the country's increasingly desperate economic plight. But the defence complex is also a powerful political force: in the view of many radical democrats it has had the government in its pocket and has used its influence to block moves towards genuinely radical reform. For patriotic conservatives, on the other hand, the erosion of the capability of the armaments industry has been seen as a betrayal of the national interest, threatening the country's security in the face of a still powerfully armed Western world. Thus the defence industry has moved to the centre of the unfolding drama of Mikhail Gorbachev's USSR.

This study attempts to cast light on the changing position of the Soviet defence industry since Gorbachev came to power in the spring of 1985. As a new communist party leader, Gorbachev was unusual in having little if any previous experience of the weapons industry. In this respect he differed greatly from Leonid Brezhnev. His lack of ties and debts to the defence industry establishment gave him a measure of freedom to take

1

steps to curb its influence. Soon it became apparent that Gorbachev had a keen appreciation of the superior capability of the military sector and that he saw the possibility of harnessing its expertise to the task of economic modernization and revitalization. First the Intermediate Nuclear Forces Treaty of 1988 and then unilateral military cuts in the following year provided opportunities to put these possibilities into practice. But it is a paradox of developments over the past five years that, far from reducing the economic power and political influence of the armaments industry, Gorbachev's actions have pushed the defence sector ever more to the centre of the stage. Initially having some freedom of action in relation to the military sector, Gorbachev has found himself ever more dependent upon it for the overall success of his policy of perestroika. Why this should be so is one of the central themes of this study.

Essential to recent developments have been the reductions in the military budget that were first announced at the end of 1988. In his historic address at the United Nations, Gorbachev reviewed the new principles of Soviet foreign policy. An interdependent world experiencing ever more pressing global problems required new concepts of security. Military might alone no longer served to ensure the security of nations. Acting in accordance with this logic, Gorbachev unveiled unilateral military cuts. The armed forces were to be reduced by 500,000 personnel; and the military budget was to be cut by 14.2 per cent over the period 1989–91, with a 19.5 per cent reduction in expenditure on weapons procurement.[1] This move was followed by the revelation of more accurate information on the scale of the budget of the Ministry of Defence. As a background to discussion of changes in the defence industry, it is helpful to review briefly the scale of the military cuts that have taken place during the past three years.

The Soviet authorities have revealed neither the true scale of military expenditure at the time at which Gorbachev became leader nor the intentions originally embodied in the five-year plan for 1986–90. For 1989 the military budget was revealed to be 77.3 billion roubles. This figure represents expenditure imputed to the Ministry of Defence; in reality much of the funding is channelled directly to the ministries of the defence industry to pay for weapons procurement and for a large proportion of the total military research and development (R&D). For 1990 the budget was reduced to 71.0 billion roubles, a cut of 8.2 per cent.

Expenditure on weapons procurement was cut from 32.6 billion roubles in the 1989 budget to 31.0 billion roubles in 1990; on military R&D, from 15.6 billion roubles to 13.2 billion roubles. Procurement and development of nuclear weapons was cut even more sharply, from 2.3 billion roubles in 1989 to 1.3 billion roubles in 1990.[2]

The budgetary process for 1991 left the armed forces with a grievance. This was the first time that the new parliamentary processes of the USSR Supreme Soviet functioned in something like a democratic manner in relation to defence expenditure. The draft military budget was considered in detail by the standing commissions of the Supreme Soviet, in particular the Committee for Questions of Defence and State Security, and the Planning, Budget and Finance Commission. The Ministry of Defence originally asked for a total budget of 66.5 billion roubles in 1990 prices, meeting the original target of a 14 per cent reduction in relation to 1989.[3] The government countered with a figure of 63.9 billion roubles, including a 23 per cent reduction in spending on R&D.[4] This R&D cut was too large for the military, who succeeded in obtaining Gorbachev's support for their cause. As a result, the Committee for Questions of Defence settled on a compromise budget of 65 billion roubles, or 98.6 billion roubles in 1991 prices.[5] Meanwhile, the Planning and Budget Commission took a firm stand on a lower figure of 96.6 billion roubles, arguing that this was all that could be afforded in circumstances of economic difficulty and budget deficit.[6] In the event, during the final stages of the budget process, the Supreme Soviet adopted this lower figure, inflicting a defeat on the military – a defeat that provoked a bitter response with charges that the country's security was being undermined.[7] The Ministry of Defence was left with the task of finding the additional 2 billion roubles savings, with the expectation that they will be made from additional cuts in procurement and, above all, R&D. The outcome is that the military budget for 1991 is not the targeted 14 per cent lower than the 1989 figure, but is at least 17 per cent lower in terms of 1990 prices. Given the increasing rate of inflation and the rising unit cost of weapons as production volumes have fallen, it is likely that the real reduction in expenditure has been even larger. This is important to establish in the light of claims in both the Soviet and the British press that the Soviet military budget increased in 1991.[8]

Information on the reduced scale of production of military hardware items is not so plentiful. There is little doubt that budget cuts, coupled with reduced exports to East European countries formerly in the Warsaw Treaty Organization, have led to lower volumes of output of many types of weapon systems. The largest reductions have probably been in the production of tanks, artillery systems, munitions, combat aircraft, some classes of missiles, and nuclear devices. In November 1990, Mikhail A. Moiseev, then chief of the general staff, revealed that deliveries of combat helicopters to the armed forces had declined by almost 60 per cent from 1988 to 1990, tanks by 40 per cent, combat aircraft by 30 per cent and munitions by 27 per cent.[9] At first it appeared that shipbuilding was to be less seriously affected, but more recent evidence suggests that this may not be the case. Cuts appear to be less severe in the fields of control and communications equipment. In addition, spending on the space programme has been trimmed. These reduced levels of output have posed increasingly urgent demands for alternative work, not only at enterprises engaged in weapons production, but also at many design and development organizations.

The chapters that follow discuss the implications of these developments for the Soviet defence industry. After an initial review of the structure of the industry and its geographical dimension, the process of conversion is considered in detail in Chapter 4. But conversion has been taking place in circumstances of economic reform and ever more forceful assertions of regional autonomy: these issues are considered in Chapter 5. As noted above, the defence industry is also an actor on the political stage: this dimension is explored in Chapter 6, which also includes discussion of the defence industry's role in the attempted coup of August 1991. The concluding chapter reviews prospects for the future and some possible implications for the West of these changes in the scale, role and operation of what was, without doubt, the most successful sector of the Soviet Union's socialist planned economy.

2
THE SOVIET DEFENCE INDUSTRY

The defence industry occupies a unique place in the Soviet economy. From the end of the 1920s to the late 1980s it enjoyed unquestioned priority. As the principal beneficiary of the centralized system of non-market, administrative allocation of resources, the military sector became the strongest, most technologically capable part of Soviet industry. Its scale, priority and dominance in the economy inevitably gave it powerful political influence. In short, the defence industry came to represent the very core of the Administrative System, the political and economic order away from which the country has been moving by hesitant steps since 1985.

Russia has a long tradition of armaments production, exemplified by the famous gun works of Tula founded in 1712. The Tsarist autocracy organized a network of state artillery works and naval shipyards; by the First World War the private manufacture of weapons was also well-established. The years of the war saw a substantial expansion of armaments production and the consolidation of modern sectors, in particular the manufacture of aircraft. In 1917, the Bolsheviks took over a sizeable and quite advanced defence industry, the factories of which were soon nationalized and placed under centralized state control. The principal arms and munitions works played a vital role during the civil war, but in the subsequent period of recovery, during the early 1920s, the defence industry did not have highest priority. This changed at the end of the decade with the adoption of the First Five-Year Plan: from then on the armaments industry began to receive ever higher priority and underwent rapid expansion and modernization.

During the 1941–5 war the weapons industry experienced dramatic change. Not only did it expand greatly in terms of numbers of enterprises, personnel and output, but it also underwent a striking geographical shift. Hundreds of enterprises were evacuated from combat zones to locations to the east of Moscow. Important centres of arms production developed in the Urals and Siberia, and to a lesser extent in Central Asia. After the war there was a brief period of reconversion to civilian production, but this process soon gave way to a renewed expansion of the defence industry as resources were allocated on a massive scale for the rapid development of nuclear weapons, missiles, jet aircraft and radar systems. This extraordinary priority for military production was checked briefly after Stalin's death, when G. M. Malenkov, the prime minister, sought to engage the defence industry in the manufacture of consumer goods. But after this short-lived episode traditional priorities were reinstated under Khrushchev and Brezhnev.

The industrial ministries
In the state-dominated, centrally planned and managed economy of the USSR the industrial ministry has been an institution of crucial importance. This is especially true of the defence industry, with its more than usually centralized administrative arrangements. Most weapons development and production has been concentrated in a group of powerful ministries representing a relatively distinct component of the industrial sector of the economy. In recent years this set of ministries has come to be known as the 'defence complex'. In addition, some military hardware and many material and equipment inputs are supplied by enterprises of other, nominally civilian, ministries. Overall administrative coordination of the defence complex and military production as a whole is undertaken by a high-level government agency, the USSR Military-Industrial Commission, often known by its Russian abbreviations, the VPK. For convenience, in the present work the term 'defence industry' refers to all military-related production carried out by Soviet industry, regardless of administrative subordination, while the term 'defence complex' refers to the group of ministries constituting the core of the weapons industry. As discussed below, the ministries of the defence complex not only manufacture armaments and other military hardware; they also have

long-established and wide-ranging civilian activities.

The administrative arrangements of the defence complex have been relatively stable during the past twenty-five years, but some partial changes were introduced in the recent period under Gorbachev. The following review relates to the situation prior to the attempted coup of August 1991, taking into account the government reorganization undertaken after the appointment of Valentin Pavlov as prime minister. Eight industrial ministries represent the core defence industry of the USSR. Formally, one of these ministries is considered to form a component of the 'fuel and energy complex', but in practice its military work is overseen by the VPK. This is the Ministry for Atomic Power and Industry – or Minatomenergoprom, as it has come to be known – which is responsible for the development and production of nuclear weapons. Given the importance of the ministries of the defence industry, there follows a brief review of the main features of each.

Minatomenergoprom was created as part of the previous government reorganization during the summer of 1989. It was formed by merging the Ministry of Medium Machinebuilding (Minsredmash), previously responsible for nuclear weapons, and the Ministry for Nuclear Power, which operated the country's civil atomic power stations. In addition, it gained control of a number of engineering works engaged in the manufacture of nuclear power equipment, including the vast 'Atommash' plant at Volgodonsk near Rostov-on-Don, built under Brezhnev for the production of reactors. The former Minsredmash owed its origins to the Soviet nuclear weapons programme led by Ivan Kurchatov. Over the years, shrouded in almost impenetrable secrecy, it became one of the country's most powerful agencies, virtually a state within the state.

The ministry is responsible for all aspects of the nuclear industry, from uranium mining and processing to the design and manufacture of nuclear bombs, warheads and other devices. It also possesses a formidable research capability, with a large network of institutes, some engaged in important fields of fundamental research, including nuclear and high-energy physics and chemistry, and more applied areas, such as industrial lasers and robotics. Its best-known research establishment is the Kurchatov Institute of Atomic Energy in Moscow, now under the directorship of Academician Evgenii Velikhov, a vice-president of the USSR Academy of Sciences. The ministry also has substantial capacity for

7

construction work both for its own needs and for outside clients. Overall, it represents one of the most powerful of all the industrial ministries of the USSR. As noted above, Minatomenergoprom has been located within the fuel and energy complex rather than the defence complex. However, this move is unlikely to have had much practical significance. It probably stemmed from a desire to at least formally emulate the arrangements of the United States, where the Department of Energy has responsibility for nuclear weapons development and production.

The Ministry of General Machinebuilding (Minobshchemash) is responsible for the development and production of most, but not all, ballistic missiles and space technology. It was the pioneering work of Sergei Korolev and his colleagues that laid the foundations of this ministry, and it is the successor to Korolev's design organization, the science-production association 'Energiya' at Kaliningrad near Moscow, that remains the basic technical centre of the Soviet space programme. Minobshchemash builds missiles, including the SS–17, –18 and –19 land-based strategic systems and major submarine-launched systems, rocket engines, control systems, launch installations and space vehicles. It also possesses a strong capability in advanced materials and production technology.

Some nuclear missiles are also built by the Ministry of the Defence Industry (Minoboronprom). The solid-fuel SS–24 and SS–25 ICBMs, plus systems that are subject to abolition under the INF Treaty, notably the SS-20, are products of this ministry, but it is better known for its conventional ground forces equipment. Of all branches of the Soviet defence industry, Minoboronprom can justly claim to have the longest tradition of weapons production. Under the ministry are some of the oldest Russian plants for the manufacture of artillery systems, small arms and ammunition, including the above-mentioned Tula gun works. Products of this ministry also include tanks and armoured vehicles, military and civil optical equipment, and a wide range of military chemical products, including explosives and rocket fuels. Finally, it possesses quite substantial capacity for the production of high-quality steels.

Between 1968 and 1989, the munitions and military chemicals industry was administered separately as the Ministry of Machinebuilding; more than 60 per cent of the ministry's enterprises were concerned with chemical products.[1] Minoboronprom has a large research capability, possessing almost a hundred research and design establishments.[2] In terms of number of facilities and personnel this is a very large ministry, employing some 2 million people in all.

While Minoboronprom takes pride in its long tradition of armaments production, the Ministry of the Aviation Industry (Minaviaprom) regards itself as one of the most capable branches of Soviet industry in terms of technology and the ability to manufacture to high standards of quality. It is also one of the largest industrial ministries: total employment is probably at least 1.75 million. According to a senior official of the ministry, in terms of employment the Soviet aviation industry is up to twice the size of its US counterpart.[3] In addition to major associations and enterprises for airframe and engine manufacture (at least twenty of the former and a dozen of the latter), the ministry has a very extensive network of factories for the production of materials, including the processing of non-ferrous metals and composites, components, instrumentation, and production equipment. The aviation industry also possesses a substantial research and design capability. Military aviation has always been the principal activity of the ministry, with civil work occupying a secondary role. Minaviaprom also has some involvement in the space programme, being responsible for the design and building of the 'Buran' space shuttle.

The Ministry of the Shipbuilding Industry is unusual in having a large proportion of its facilities located in Leningrad, with other major centres in the Southern Ukraine and the Far East. The dominant position of Leningrad is shown by the fact that 70 per cent of the ministry's R&D establishments are found there.[4] It is a large ministry, having 350 factories, including 70 shipyards.[5] Like the aviation industry, it has a strong bias towards military work.

The remaining three ministries of the defence complex are all concerned with electronics-related activities. It is a striking feature of Soviet industrial development in the postwar period that the new industries associated with electronics have been concentrated heavily in the military sector. Indeed, a strong case can be advanced that it is precisely this one-sided pattern of development that has been responsible for the current backwardness of the civil electronics and information technology industries.

The oldest ministry in this sector, and the one with the highest prestige, is the Ministry of the Radio Industry (Minradprom). This branch has its origins in the wartime development of military radio and radar. Later, in the postwar years, it was Minradprom that had prime responsibility for the development of mainframe general-purpose computers. In terms of employment and number of facilities, it is without doubt a very large ministry with an exceptionally strong research capability: according to the former minister, Vladimir I. Shimko, R&D in the branch employs more than 300,000 people.[6] Today the ministry's principal activities are the production of radar systems, radio equipment, anti-aircraft and anti-missile systems, computers, control and navigation systems, and a wide range of consumer goods, including radios, record players and televisions.

The supply of electronic components is a near monopoly of the Ministry of the Electronics Industry (Minelektronprom). The fact that component supply has been retained within the defence complex provides strong evidence of the military orientation of the industry. In terms of output, Minelektronprom has been the fastest-growing of all industrial ministries and, because of the nature of the technology, has been forced to devote serious attention to the effective organization and management of research and innovation. The principal research centre of the ministry is located at Zelenograd, a satellite town of Moscow. Over time the ministry has steadily expanded its range of end-products, which now include microcomputers, lasers and many consumer items. The near-monopoly position of the ministry has given it considerable power and influence, and it is not surprising that in recent years other ministries have sought to develop their own component manufacture.

The final ministry of the defence complex underwent substantial reorganization following the government changes in the summer of 1989. The new Ministry of Communications (Minsvyaz') was created as a result of a merger between much of the former Ministry of Communications Equipment (Minpromsvyaz') and the pre-existing communications ministry. This vast conglomerate ministry, the responsibilities of which included not only the manufacture of communications equipment, but also the Soviet telephone and postal services, employed about 2.5 million people.[7] It is thus a curious feature of Soviet reality that the entire postal system is now formally part of the defence complex. In 1991 facilities responsible for the development and manufacture of telephone equipment were hived off from the ministry to form a new independent concern, 'Telekom'.

Most nominally civilian ministries also have some involvement in military production and therefore form part of the defence industry according to the broader definition adopted here. In particular, this applies to enterprises of the civilian machinebuilding complex, which supply military trucks, armoured vehicles, diesel engines, electrical equipment and control instruments. Enterprises of the chemical and petrochemical industries supply fuels and lubricants, materials and tyres. The Ministry of Metallurgy also has a major role as supplier of ferrous and non-ferrous metals. The contribution of some consumer-related industries should also not be overlooked. Enterprises of light industry supply not only uniforms and footwear for the forces, but also parachutes.

During recent years there has been a policy of reducing the number of industrial ministries through mergers and by transforming them into commercially orientated associations and concerns that are outside the formal structures of government. In particular this has applied to the civilian machinebuilding industry: under Brezhnev there were eleven ministries, now only two remain, with general oversight the responsibility of a State Committee for Machinebuilding, the chairman of which, Genrikh Stroganov, was formerly deputy minister of the aviation industry. With the establishment of the new Cabinet of Ministers in 1991, although at one time there was a hint that the aviation and missile industries were to be merged, the defence-complex ministries were left intact. The reluctance to restructure the defence industry meant that its ministries came to represent an ever larger proportion of the total number of industrial ministries: under Brezhnev approximately one-quarter of the total; under Pavlov, more than half. This shift may have served to enhance the influence of the military sector in the USSR government.

The scale of the defence industry
The scale of the defence complex, and the defence industry as a whole, is not easy to determine with any accuracy. During the past two to three years, glasnost has improved our knowledge of many aspects of the Soviet military effort, but to only a limited extent has it provided reliable, unambiguous data on the scale of the armaments industry. The situation

has been further complicated by the administrative changes in industry that have taken place since 1988. However, from the fragmentary information available, it is possible to generate reasonably reliable estimates of the scale of military production and of the defence complex in terms of output, capital stock, employment and, less reliably, the number of establishments.

This is not the place for detailed statistical analysis: the following in part summarizes evidence assembled by the author and presented in more detail elsewhere.[8] In all estimates of the scale of the defence industry in terms of output and capital stock there is a fundamental problem: the price relatives prevailing in the Soviet economy provide a distorted view of reality, and the systematic bias is in the direction of understatement of the scale of the military sector. The following output estimates are based on Soviet current prices before the major price revision of January 1991. For the capital stock there is no alternative but to use the so-called comparable prices employed in Soviet statistics. In so far as advanced domestically produced equipment installed in the defence industry is underpriced, this will again provide a distorted picture.

On the basis of data for 1988, it can be estimated that the defence complex as it was then constituted employed approximately 7.5 million industrial production personnel, of whom some 4.1 million were engaged in the manufacture of weapons and other military hardware. The total gross output of the complex was more than 140 billion roubles, of which the military component was approximately 88 billion roubles. Thus the defence complex alone accounts for one-fifth of the total industrial labour force and about 16 per cent of gross industrial output. The capital stock of the complex is valued at approximately 115 billion roubles, about 12 per cent of the total in industry. However, it must be noted that an important issue remains unclear: the data for the defence complex on which the above estimates are based may exclude much, and possibly all, of the employment of the nuclear industry, in particular those engaged in the production of nuclear weapons.

For a more complete picture, account must also be taken of the weapons and military hardware production undertaken outside the defence complex. According to data supplied by the USSR to the International Labour Office, in 1988 this component of the armaments industry employed almost 550,000 industrial production personnel.[9] It can be estimated that military output of these workers was approximately 9 billion roubles. Thus, total employment in the manufacture of weapons and military hardware in 1988 was approximately 4.7 million (13 per cent of the total industrial labour force), and total gross output was almost 100 billion roubles (11 per cent of industrial production). The estimate of defence industry employment offered here is similar to totals recently published elsewhere: 4.8 million according to a Soviet source, and more than 5 million in an authoritative Western report.[10] The question of definition of employment is important. The 7.5 and 4.7 million refer to the standard Soviet statistical category 'industrial production personnel'. However, this is not the same as the total number of people employed by industrial ministries. First, it excludes those employed in independent research institutes and design organizations. Second, it excludes those engaged in construction, agriculture, transport and other non-industrial productive activities. Third, it does not include all those working in health clinics, sanatoria, holiday homes and the many other ancilliary activities typical of a Soviet industrial ministry. Given that strong emphasis on such social and cultural provision is known to be a feature of the defence sector, it is likely that this extra employment is large. The industrial ministries of the defence complex could therefore employ as many as 12 million people, a substantial labour force, but, to put it in proportion, less than 10 per cent of the total number employed in the economy.[11]

It is not so easy to determine the number of production and research establishments of the defence complex. Over recent years there has been an active 'merger' movement in Soviet industry, involving the grouping of enterprises into production associations and science-production associations (hereafter designated PO and NPO respectively, according to the usual Soviet initials). The NPO are centred on research institutes or design organizations. These associations may be quite large: in the early 1980s in the Ministry of the Electronics Industry an association contained on average 6.2 enterprises (including 5.3 per PO and 9.1 per NPO).[12] Some evidence for the non-electronics ministries suggests that a smaller number of enterprises per association may be more typical. Further complications arise from the changing administrative boundaries of the defence complex, and also the transfer to it of civilian enterprises, which has been a feature of recent years.

According to the former prime minister, Nikolai Ryzhkov, the defence complex has more than 400 enterprises not connected with the production of military technology.[13] Valentin I. Smyslov, the first deputy of the former State Planning Committee (Gosplan), who is responsible for defence-sector planning, claims that approximately 20 per cent of defence-complex enterprises are engaged solely in civilian production, including not only facilities transferred in the recent period, but also established enterprises for metallurgy, machine tools and other non-weapons production.[14] This suggests a total of approximately 2,000 associations and enterprises, of which some 1,600 are involved in military production.[15] Many of the 1,600 facilities will be associations, each embracing two or more enterprises. This is compatible with the suggestion by a Soviet specialist that there are some 5,000 enterprises within the military sector.[16]

The defence complex plays a substantial role in Soviet R&D. Its institutes and design organizations not only undertake R&D for the creation of new military hardware, but perform civil R&D, including basic scientific research. Indeed, this basic research is second only to that undertaken by the USSR Academy of Sciences. The evidence suggests that in 1988 the ministries of the defence complex undertook three-quarters of total Soviet industrial R&D. Within the complex, more than 70 per cent of the R&D was military in character, but the remaining 30 per cent represented almost half of all the country's civil industrial research, indicating that even before conversion the defence industry made a major contribution to the development of civil technology.[17] As for the number of research institutes and design organizations, a very approximate estimate suggests as many as 600–800 establishments.

The administrative apparatus of the defence industry
As noted above, administrative oversight of the defence sector is exercised by the VPK, a supra-ministerial organization headed by a deputy prime minister. Until the government reorganization of early 1991, it was headed by Igor S. Belousov, who, prior to his appointment in 1988, served as minister of the shipbuilding industry. In January 1991 Belousov was replaced by Yurii D. Maslyukov. This was an interesting career move in so far as Maslyukov had already chaired the VPK during the

early Gorbachev period, 1985–8, before becoming head of Gosplan. The background to this appointment was revealed by Gorbachev at the time when he proposed Pavlov for the post of prime minister. It emerged that Gorbachev had first offered the post to Maslyukov, but he had expressed a preference for leadership of the defence industry – probably a shrewd choice in view of the accelerating collapse of the economy![18] Under Maslyukov were a first deputy (Vladimir L. Koblov) and five or six deputy chairmen. The deputies have responsibility for the oversight of particular fields of military production. An important body is the VPK's Scientific and Technical Council, currently chaired by Anatolii V. Kulakov, a corresponding member of the USSR Academy of Sciences. The Council plays a major role in the selection, approval and monitoring of military R&D projects. No details have been published, but it is likely that the VPK is a quite substantial administrative body, equivalent in size to an industrial ministry. Only one institute has been officially acknowledged as belonging to the VPK: the Central Research Institute for Economics and Conversion, organized in 1990. Following the failed coup attempt in August 1991, Arkadii Volsky, a member of the interim economic committee, took over responsibility for oversight of the defence industry. At the time of writing the future of the VPK remains uncertain.

In the planning and management of the military sector the VPK used to work closely with Gosplan. Within Gosplan there were sub-departments, specialized by branch of the defence industry, and an overall summary department for the defence complex, headed by Yurii A. Glybin. Overall leadership of Gosplan's military work was exercised by one of its first deputy chairmen, most recently Smyslov. Early in 1991 Gosplan was effectively disbanded as an independent organization, being absorbed into a new Ministry of Economics and Forecasting headed by First Deputy Prime Minister Vladimir Shcherbakov. The departments for the defence complex were retained, but were merged with those for the civil machinebuilding industry, a move designed to overcome what Shcherbakov has termed the 'oasis' state of the defence industry.[19] Other economic agencies can be expected to have special departments for the defence sector, including the Ministry of Material Resources (formerly the State Committee for Material and Technical Supply), the Committee for Prices (which became a subdivision of the Ministry of Economics),

15

the Ministry for Labour and Social Questions and the Ministry of Finance. However, it is possible that some functions are handled by the VPK itself, without the involvement of the relevant government bodies. This certainly applies in the field of science and technology: the State Committee for Science and Technology has no direct involvement in military-related R&D.[20]

The administrative elite of the defence industry deserves special consideration. The top ministerial officials are almost invariably of a common background. As a general rule they are engineers, graduates of one of the country's elite technical institutes, who have risen from the shop floor or lower managerial positions to become enterprise or institute directors for a number of years before entering the ministerial apparatus. It is also quite common for members of this group to have switched for a period to a communist party post, before returning to resume their industrial careers. Analysis by the author of the backgrounds of 36 leading occupants of top administrative posts in the defence complex between 1965 and 1987 revealed that all were Russians except two of Ukrainian background. All had higher education; strongly represented were graduates of the Leningrad Mechanical Institute, Leningrad Shipbuilding Institute, Moscow Bauman Technical Institute, Moscow University, Moscow Energy Institute and the Urals Polytechnic Institute. One-third graduated from Leningrad institutes, the same proportion as from Moscow higher educational establishments.[21]

The scientific and technical elite of the defence industry also have characteristics in common. An analysis of the backgrounds of 63 prominent specialists associated with the military sector revealed that 86 per cent were Russian. Only one was a Jew, Academician Yu. B. Khariton, for more than forty years scientific leader of the country's principal nuclear weapons R&D centre, Arzamas–16. Of the 60 with higher education, more than 60 per cent graduated from only six elite establishments, including eleven from the Moscow Aviation Institute and a further eight from the Bauman Institute. The other four were the Leningrad Polytechnic Institute, Moscow University, Moscow Energy Institute and the Zhu-kovskii Military Aviation Institute. Until recently it was a normal expectation that leading specialists of the defence industry would gain election to the USSR Academy of Sciences: 80 per cent of the sample were full or corresponding members. Although some of the older-generation specialists did not join the communist party, membership became normal for all those rising to prominence in the Brezhnev years, just as it was for all the administrative elite.[22] Those rising to the top as administrators or technical specialists could also expect to receive the highest state awards: the title Hero of Socialist Labour and the Order of Lenin.

There is no doubt that the administrative elite of the defence industry consists of some of the most competent and experienced administrators in the Soviet economy. They have achieved the most substantial results within the terms of the traditional administrative-command system. The available published evidence, supported by the author's own impressions gained from personal contact with top officials of the Military-Industrial Commission and of the defence-complex ministries, points to a well-established administrative culture, characterized by an ethic of hard work, long working hours, limited leisure and holidays, and a relatively modest, at times almost ascetic, style of personal life. This has been an administrative elite highly conscious of its responsibility for the country's national security. It is understandable that the former prime minister, Ryzhkov, himself of similar background, should have held this group in high regard. In his words, they constituted a special group, 'an elite' standing 'a head taller than the rest'.[23] However, as will be discussed, in Soviet society at large there is a widely held view that this 'elite' is of conservative disposition, hostile to radical economic transformation and democratization.

Within the defence complex, a special place has been occupied by the industry producing nuclear weapons. The former Minsredmash worked in conditions of exceptional secrecy. In this closed world the administrative-command system was secured the most favourable conditions for its successful operation. As a Soviet author observes, it gained from being so self-contained, since it was cut off to such an extent from the civilian economy that it hardly experienced any of its problems. This industry, it is claimed, during all its existence never once failed to fulfil the state plan. The ministry's personnel, the *sredmashevtsy*, take pride in their discipline and order. 'As a matter of fact,' the author concludes, 'in Sredmash is concentrated today the intellectual, engineering, and business elite of our society.'[24] As economic disintegration gathered pace, it is not surprising that this defence-industry elite began to be seen by some as a last bastion of order; or that some of the elite itself should have arrived at the same conclusion.

3

THE GEOGRAPHY OF THE DEFENCE INDUSTRY

Conversion and problems of economic reform at a local level have focused attention on the geographical location of the production and research facilities of the defence industry. It is evident that some cities and regions of the USSR face acute problems arising from the dominance of their local economies by military enterprises. Previously secret 'closed' towns are emerging from the shadows, attempting to adapt to the new conditions of conversion and of economic and political change. Unfortunately, data on the geography and scale of the Soviet defence industry remain sparse: an adequate view can be obtained only by indirect means.

Over several years, the author has assembled a database on enterprises and research establishments of the defence industry.[1] The sample is sufficiently large to permit a detailed analysis of the regional distribution of the facilities of the defence-sector ministries. This evidence has been supplemented by data from the Soviet statistical agency, Goskomstat. It must be stressed that the findings are provisional, subject to revision as more evidence becomes available.[2]

The sample analysed includes 550 production associations and enterprises, 97 science-production associations (NPO), 84 independent research institutes and 29 design organizations, giving a total of 760 facilities of the defence complex. Since most of the NPO are based on research institutes, often of great importance, they are included for purposes of analysis together with the other institutes, giving a total of 210 R&D organizations in the sample. Although the sample is believed to

The share of the defence complex in total industrial employment by economic region of the USSR

Share

Low
Low–Medium
Medium
Medium–High
High

be reasonably representative of the defence complex as a whole, the nature of the sources used probably leads to an overstatement of the importance of Moscow and Leningrad, and an understatement of the significance of the Urals region.

Of the total number of production and R&D facilities in the sample, 75.1 per cent are located in the Russian Soviet Federal Socialist Republic (including 71.6 per cent of enterprises and 84.3 per cent of R&D establishments), 14.5 per cent in the Ukraine (16.7 and 8.6 per cent), 2.5 per cent in Belorussia (2.9 and 1.4 per cent) and the remaining 7.9 per cent in the other 12 republics, including 2.9 per cent in the Baltic republics. This shows clearly the predominant role of Russia and the Ukraine.

An interesting feature of the overall geographical distribution is the wider diffusion of production facilities associated with the newer, electronics-related branches of the defence complex, in comparison with the more traditional, mechanical branches. Taking enterprises of the ministries of the electronics industry, the radio industry and communications to represent the former, and the other defence industry ministries to represent the latter, the following picture emerges. Of the total number of production and research facilities of the 'electronic' branches, 65 per cent are located in the RSFSR, compared with 82 per cent of the facilities of the 'mechanical' industries. For the Ukraine, the shares are 17.2 and 12.7 per cent respectively; and for Belorussia 5.8 and 0.2 per cent. The shares of the remaining republics are 12.3 and 4.8 per cent, including 5.5 and 1.0 per cent for the Baltic republics. More detailed analysis suggests that, for the newer, electronics-related sector of the defence complex, the availability of plentiful, predominantly female, labour for the assembly operations has been an important consideration in shaping location patterns.

It is the main end-product weapons plants and their associated R&D establishments that are located overwhelmingly in the Russian republic. Of the facilities identified as being under the Ministry of the Defence Industry (including munitions), 88 per cent are located in the RSFSR; of the missile-building Ministry of General Machinebuilding, 81 per cent; of the aviation industry ministry, 90 per cent; and of the shipbuilding industry, 72 per cent (plus 22 per cent in the Ukraine).

Supplementing the database of organizations with information on the structure of employment, it is possible to identify those regions with unusually high concentrations of defence-complex employment.[3] For statistical purposes the USSR State Committee for Statistics divides the country into economic regions. The regions with the highest proportions of employment in defence-complex enterprises and associations appear to be the Northwest, Urals, Volgo-Vyatka and Volga regions of the RSFSR, and the southern region of the Ukraine, notable for its shipbuilding (see map).

More detailed analysis by individual *oblasti* (regions), autonomous republics and major cities indicates the principal centres of defence-complex employment. In terms of the absolute number employed in production, the top ten localities appear to be Sverdlovsk, Leningrad (city), Moscow (city), Nizhnii-Novgorod (Gor'kii), Moscow (*oblast'*), Perm', Samara (Kuibyshev), Novosibirsk, Tatarstan (Tatar ASSR) and the Udmurtiya (Udmurt ASSR).[4] These are all within the Russian republic. In terms of the share of the defence complex in total employment (industrial production personnel only), a somewhat different picture emerges. The ten *oblasti* with the highest shares appear to be the Udmurtiya, Nikolaev (southern Ukraine), Kaluga (southwest of Moscow), Mariiel (Marii ASSR), northern Kazakhstan, Omsk, Voronezh, Novgorod (a centre of the electronics industry), Perm' and Vladimir. This analysis indicates those localities likely to experience particular difficulties from defence cuts and conversion.

For R&D, the evidence of the database of establishments indicates the dominant position of Moscow. The capital possesses some 40 per cent of all identified R&D organizations, followed by Leningrad (about 20 per cent), the Moscow region (5 per cent), Kiev, Novosibirsk and Nizhnii-Novgorod. The predominance of Moscow requires some qualification, however, since many of its institutes have branch organizations in other localities, and it has not proved possible to take them into account. The existence of branch R&D organizations means that the spread of employment in defence-complex research is less concentrated than the above-cited proportions suggest.

Although the RSFSR dominates the Soviet defence industry, other republics also possess important facilities. In terms of end-product weapons, it is only the Ukraine that has a major production capability. The principal centres are Kiev, which also has a number of important research facilities, Khar'kov (including a sizeable tank plant), Dnepropetrovsk (with a substantial facility for strategic missiles), Lugansk (Voroshilovgrad), L'vov (notable for its electronics-related industry) and, in the south, the naval shipbuilding of Nikolaev and the Crimea. Minsk is the principal centre in Belorussia, but overall the republic does not play a very significant role.

Kazakhstan not only has a number of important production facilities, especially in its northern region; it is also the location of some of the USSR's major test sites for armaments. Under Ministry of Defence control, these sites include the nuclear weapons test site near Semipalatinsk, the Sary Shagan range for air defence systems, and the Baikonur (Tyuratam) space and missile centre. According to Kazakh claims, there are eight weapons test sites in the republic, occupying 18 million hectares, or almost 7 per cent, of its territory.[5] This represents 40 per cent of the total territory of the USSR occupied by Ministry of Defence test sites.[6]

In the Central Asian republics, both Uzbekistan and Kyrgyzstan (Kirgizia) possess facilities of some significance, notably centres of the nuclear industry involved in uranium mining and processing, but also a growing number of enterprises concerned with electronics-related production. Of the Transcaucasian republics, both Georgia and Armenia have production and research establishments of some importance. Again, electronics-related activities are well-represented, together with, in Georgia, the aircraft and shipbuilding industries. The three Baltic republics also have defence industry involvement of some note. Electronics-related production and research predominate, but Estonia, a republic with a uranium industry, possesses in addition a number of facilities of the nuclear industry. The republics of Azerbaidzhan, Turkmenistan, Tadzhikistan and Moldova (Moldavia) do not appear to contribute much to the defence industry.

This overall view of the location of the Soviet defence industry can be supplemented by more detailed information on individual towns and regions. Moscow and Leningrad are both extremely important centres. Not only is Moscow the administrative centre of the Soviet defence industry; it is also the principal centre for research and design organizations, especially of the aerospace industry. Half of all the applied R&D performed in the city is undertaken by the defence sector. Military production accounts for a third of the city's industrial output and employs one-quarter of the labour force.[7] Around Moscow there are satellite towns dominated by particular branches of the defence industry. Examples include Zelenograd, the country's principal research centre of the microelectronics industry, a town of 160,000, with a labour force of some 100,000, almost half scientists and other specialists, most of whom are employed at institutes and enterprises of the NPO 'Nauchnyi Tsentr' of Minelektronprom.[8] Similarly, Kaliningrad (Podlipki) near Moscow is an important research centre of the missile-space industry, and Zhukovskii a centre of the aviation industry.[9]

In Leningrad some 700,000 people work in the defence industry, a quarter of the total number employed in the city.[10] Strongly represented are the shipbuilding, radio and ground-forces equipment industries; and to a lesser extent the missile and aviation industries. Overall, Leningrad has approximately 150 enterprises and 26 research institutes of the defence complex.[11]

The economies of certain towns and regions are dominated by military-related production. Examples include Tula, Chelyabinsk, Sverdlovsk, Biisk in Siberia, Kovrov (where, it has been claimed, the military sector accounts for nearly 90 per cent of the town's industry), Perm' (with a claimed 70 per cent military share of manufacturing output) and Sverdlovsk (with a 40 per cent share of military output).[12] An extraordinary concentration of defence plants is also found in the Udmurtiya. All the important towns – Izhevsk, Votkinsk, Sarapul and Glazov – are dominated by defence industry facilities. Military production is reported to account for an astonishing 85 per cent of the republic's total industrial output and some 60 per cent of total employment.[13] The defence industry is also strongly represented in other formerly Autonomous Republics of Russia, notably Mariiel and Tartarstan; in the case of Mariiel, it has been claimed that 80 per cent of industrial production is for defence.[14]

In some relatively remote locations there are whole communities built around defence production centres. Examples include the northern town of Severodvinsk, the location of the world's largest facility for building submarines, and Shevchenko on the shores of the Caspian sea, a town serving a vast complex of the uranium industry. The towns of Zheltye Vody in the Ukraine, Stepnogorsk in Kazakhstan, and Navoi in Uzbekistan are similarly dominated by uranium mining and processing, being effectively 'ministry towns' of the former Ministry of Medium

Machinebuilding. Until recently, such centres have often been 'closed' towns, with restricted access not only to foreigners, but also to Soviet citizens. Since recent developments have impinged so acutely on these closed centres, they deserve special consideration.

Closed towns

During the past three years in the Soviet Union the existence of closed towns has been openly acknowledged for the first time. Most of those revealed have been associated with nuclear weapons research and production. In its early years, under Stalin, the ultra-secret nuclear weapons programme was overseen by Lavrentii Beria. The construction of industrial and research facilities involved many prisoners from the labour camp system. In the post-Stalin years, the nuclear programme continued to receive the highest state priority, and the Ministry of Medium Machinebuilding, charged with running the nuclear industry, became an extremely powerful organization under the leadership of its minister, Efim Slavskii. The creation of closed towns was not only a means of maintaining a regime of extraordinary secrecy; it also permitted the establishment of relatively privileged conditions, concealed from public view, for those working 'beyond the barbed wire'. It is likely that this archipelago of closed communities has a total population of several hundred thousand people, including some of the country's most able scientists and engineers; but the towns are not to be found on any Soviet maps.

The most famous closed facility is probably Chelyabinsk–40, near Kyshtym, the location of the Soviet Union's first industrial reactor for the production of weapons-grade plutonium. This is the location of the 'Mayak' association, which when in full operation had six working reactors and a chemical separation plant. Nearby is the town of Chelyabinsk–65 (at one time known as Beria), most of whose 80,000 inhabitants work at 'Mayak'.[15] North of the town of Kasli is Chelyabinsk–70, the location of the country's second research facility for the design of nuclear weapons, the All-Union Research Institute of Technical Physics, established in the mid-1950s.[16]

Another notable closed town is Arzamas–16, the country's principal research centre for nuclear weapons, founded in 1946 at the historic Sarov monastery near Arzamas in Nizhnii-Novgorod (Gor'kii) *oblast'*.

Several thousand people are employed at the All-Union Research Institute of Experimental Physics (VNIIEF) – the famous 'installation' of Andrei Sakharov's memoirs – and other facilities of this closed town. Until it was declassified in November 1990 it was one of the most highly secret locations of the country.[17] Krasnoyarsk–45 (or Krasnoyarsk–9 as it is sometimes called) is a closed town established in the 1950s on the Enisei river to the east of Krasnoyarsk as a centre for the production of plutonium for nuclear weapons. It also became the location of an important facility of the missile/space industry concerned with satellite systems, the NPO 'prikladnoi mekhaniki' under the leadership of Academician M. F. Reshetnev. Krasnoyarsk–45 has now been opened up, with access permitted to foreigners.[18] Nearby is Krasnoyarsk–26, the location of a nuclear processing plant now undergoing conversion.[19]

Yet another closed town of the nuclear weapons industry is Tomsk-7 (Severskii), the location of 'Sibkhimkombinat', the 'Siberian nuclear power station', a complex of reactors and processing plant dating from the early 1950s. This town of 100,000 people has also now received its first foreign visitors.[20] Near the Semipalatinsk nuclear weapons test site is the closed town of Kurchatov (Semipalatinsk–21), with nuclear research facilities of Minatomenergoprom.[21] Similar closed towns were built to serve the space programme, e.g. Leninsk near the Baikonur (Tyuratam) cosmodrome in Kazakhstan and Mirnyi near the Plesetsk launch site in the northern Arkhangel'skaya *oblast*. In time it is likely that more closed towns will be opened to public view, some of them after decades of secret existence.

With borders guarded by the internal troops, these secret 'zones' have provided a remarkably sheltered existence. Until recently, when some closed towns have begun to open up, their inhabitants had no access to the normal telephone network and were not allowed to publish a local newspaper. Unless essential for work purposes, movement beyond the bounds of the zone was discouraged, to the extent that financial rewards were offered to those spending their annual holidays at home. Even the closest relatives were permitted to visit at most once a year at the discretion of those responsible for the very strict security regime. Foreign travel was forbidden, as was any contact with foreigners. On the other hand, the closed towns were developed so as to provide relatively privileged conditions to compensate for their isolation. The available evidence suggests they were well provided with housing, social ammenities and well-stocked shops. Pay was good and many workers retired early, at 50 or 55, in recognition of the hazardous nature of the nuclear-related work. The directors of these secret facilities were all-powerful, backed up by the immense resources of Minsredmash. Some simultaneously served as town mayors. I. N. Bortnikov, who served as director of one closed installation for twenty years, has been described as 'tsar and god' of the closed town, within which 'he built his own communism'.[22]

Accounts of closed towns stress that until recently all who lived and worked there willingly accepted the privations involved, since they recognized the vital necessity of their work for the maintenance of Soviet national security, as well as appreciating the privileges they received in compensation. There was no difficulty in attracting the best graduates of the elite educational institutes. In conditions of military cuts and conversion, plus the post-Chernobyl downgrading of civil nuclear power, this and other aspects of life in the 'zones' is undergoing change. As discussed in Chapter 4, the *esprit de corps* is weakening, privileges are being eroded, and one of the few remaining advantages of life 'beyond the barbed wire' is the low level of crime and social problems.

It is not only closed towns that have restricted access to foreign visitors; many cities and regions important for military production have also denied their inhabitants contact with the outside world. During 1990 a number of newly elected local councils began to appeal to the USSR and republican governments, asking for permission to open up their towns and regions. In December 1990, the USSR Council of Ministers decided to ease restrictions to the extent that the proportion of 'closed' territory in the Soviet Union has been reduced from 11 per cent to 6.3 per cent. Towns that were opened up include Kaliningrad, Krasnoyarsk, Samara (Kuibyshev), Magadan, Norilsk, Omsk, Sverdlovsk and Tomsk, plus Udmurtiya and parts of the Ukraine and the Far East.[23] However, information on the opening-up of Krasnoyarsk indicates that unrestricted access is not envisaged. Foreigners will be able to visit by invitation only and the ruling does not extend to Krasnoyarsk–9 and other satellite towns of the city.[24]

Notwithstanding the high priority of the defence industry, towns and regions dominated by military-related production can experience serious difficulties. One-sided emphasis on defence can be associated with serious neglect of consumer goods production, services and other amenities. Formerly, the mechanisms of planned distribution could ensure that such localities were provided with adequate supplies of food and consumer goods; now, as economic dislocation intensifies, the traditional protective mechanisms are breaking down, which is giving rise to serious problems and exacerbating the difficulties created by cuts and conversion.

Environmental hazards

Localities with defence industry plants are liable to experience serious environmental and safety hazards. In the past these issues were kept secret – even major nuclear incidents like the disaster at Chelyabinsk–40 were never officially acknowledged. This has now changed, giving rise to a series of revelations of accidents and environmental harm. The Chernobyl disaster focused attention on the shortcomings of the nuclear industry, but this incident was only one of a long chain.[25] One of the most recent involved the Ust'–Kamenogorsk 'Ul'binskii metallurgicheskii zavod' in Kazakhstan. This facility for the production of beryllium, tantalum and nuclear fuel materials is located in the centre of the town, which suffered serious pollution following an explosion at the works in September 1990.[26] But nuclear-related hazards are not restricted to the atomic weapons industry. It has been alleged that in the vicinity of Severodvinsk, the principal centre for the construction of nuclear submarines, the surrounding territory and coastal waters have been subject to radioactive pollution.[27]

Another industry with a very bad record is that of explosives and conventional munitions, which is now under the Ministry of the Defence Industry. During the past two years, this industry has had an appalling record of accidents, which are no longer concealed from the public. Works involved include the Pavlograd chemical works in the Ukraine, site of two serious explosions within eighteen months; the Gorlovko works in the Donbass, responsible for widescale pollution of local coal mines with dangerous chemicals; the Biisk 'oleumnyi zavod' in Siberia, where an explosion caused eleven fatalities; and a chemical works near Asbest in the Sverdlovsk region, which also experienced an explosion.[28] Accident investigations often reveal poor observance of technical procedures and lax management. The mounting evidence indicates that for many years, behind an almost impenetrable cloak of secrecy, the defence industry has been operating with shocking disregard for safety.[29] The national industrial safety inspectorate, now Gospromatomnadzor, was denied access to defence plants, and statistics on accidents were never revealed.[30] But the recent spate of incidents has finally prompted government action. Gospromatomnadzor has been granted access to 27 chemical-related plants producing explosive products belonging to the Ministry of the Defence Industry. It soon became apparent to the workers of this civil agency that the plants concerned had been devoting all their resources to product improvement, leaving no money for safety measures. Under the new regime, management will be obliged to observe the strict rules enforced by the inspectorate. The nuclear and missile ministries have now also expressed willingness for some of their chemical plants to come under civil safety control.[31]

An interesting issue, not easily explored, is the influence of the geography of the defence industry on local politics. Do those cities and regions with large concentrations of military enterprises and research establishments have their own distinct political colour? Are they inclined to conservatism, to the defence of traditional Soviet values, with emphasis on the maintenance of the union and an ordered, state-dominated, centrally managed economy? Unfortunately, until recently, access to the local press of such localities has been tightly restricted, limiting the available evidence. We return to this issue in Chapter 6.

4

CONVERSION: STRATEGY AND PRACTICE

From the outset Mikhail Gorbachev made clear his belief that the defence industry should contribute to the revitalization of the civilian economy. At first regarded as a potential aid to industrial modernization, defence-sector reorientation began increasingly to be seen as vital to achieving a short-term amelioration of the living standards of the Soviet people. At the same time, there has been growing recognition at both elite and popular levels that the Soviet Union possesses a hypertrophied arma-ments industry, the one-sided, priority development of which has contrib-uted in no small part to the country's parlous economic state. Now, as defence expenditure is being cut back, there is growing pressure for a decisive demilitarization of the Soviet economy.

Gorbachev came to power remarkably free from defence-sector ties. With the break-up of the formerly dominant Ustinov group of defence-industry leaders, who had had close links with Brezhnev, political condi-tions were created that were favourable to the sector's reorientation.[1] Since 1985, there have been several strands to the policy of engaging the military sector in the task of economic renewal. With Nikolai Ryzhkov as prime minister, leading administrative personnel of the defence industry were switched to prominent government posts, taking responsibility for important areas of the civilian economy. The long-established civilian activities of defence-sector enterprises have been given new emphasis. Production capacity, vital for meeting the population's consumption and welfare needs, has been transferred to the defence industry for rapid modernization and expansion of output. Efforts have also been made to promote technology transfer and spin-off to the civilian economy, and, with reduced outlays on defence, a process of partial conversion from military to civilian production has been initiated.

Long before the current policy of conversion, the Soviet defence industry had an extensive civilian involvement.[2] Enterprises of the defence complex produced a wide range of industrial and transport equipment, including machine tools, oil-drilling rigs and rail freight wagons, in addition to civil aircraft and ships, most of the country's output of electronic goods, computers and communications equipment, tractors and agricultural machinery, some chemical products, and a substantial volume of consumer goods. Not only were enterprises of the defence industry responsible for the manufacture of the country's entire output of television sets, radios and cameras, but they also accounted for between a third and two-thirds of all refrigerators, washing-machines, vacuum cleaners, bicycles and motor cycles. Although the quality of these goods lagged behind the best world standards, it was generally superior to the level attained by enterprises of civilian branches of industry. Civil production was widely diffused within the defence complex: most enterprises had some involvement, and their directors became accustomed to periodic communist party campaigns to boost their contribution to the population's living-standards and welfare.

A significant milestone in the evolution of policy was a decision adopted towards the end of 1987 that the modernization of the food industry and many enterprises manufacturing consumer goods would best be achieved by transferring prime responsibility for the development and building of appropriate production equipment to the ministries of the defence industry. At about the time the new policy was adopted, Gorbachev visited an exhibition of food-processing equipment, where he examined machines built by the Leningrad 'Kirovskii zavod' and other defence enterprises, and was, apparently, favourably impressed, suggesting his active involvement in the decision. Later, however, at the 28th Communist Party Congress in 1990, the former Politburo member Aleksandra Biryukova, in charge of social policy, claimed personal credit for the policy initiative.[3] Be that as it may, in the spring of 1988 the defence sector acquired 230 enterprises from the disbanded Ministry of Machinebuilding for the Light and Food Industries. Generally poorly equipped, the enterprises employed more than 300,000 workers and had an annual output of some 5 billion roubles and a 1987 profit of 738 million roubles.[4] Among the factories were many producers of consumer durables, giving the defence industry a near monopoly in the manufacture of refrigerators, washing-machines, sewing-machines and other household goods. Many of the enterprises were quickly absorbed into existing production associations of the defence complex and have effectively disappeared as independent entities.

At a stroke, the defence industry was forced to take on new responsibilities, and it is hardly surprising that many problems have been encountered. The inherited facilities required extensive modernization, and many of their products were technologically backward. The government adopted ambitious programmes for the production of equipment for the food and light industries, and also for the retail trade and public catering, leaving the defence-complex ministries with little choice but to utilize some of their basic facilities. The personnel of many leading design organizations and enterprises, lacking any previous experience, found themselves suddenly required to produce machinery for the food-processing and consumer industries. Moreover, they had to adapt to the new experience of working for relatively weak and ill-informed customers. By early 1989 it was claimed that 345 basic enterprises and 205 research and design establishments had become involved.[5] But not all the customers have appreciated the change. Improvements in the quality of the equipment built have been slow to appear, and prices have frequently risen sharply, prompting complaints of 'direct financial aggression' exerted by military producers.[6] Despite frequent protests and appeals to the government, this problem has not only persisted, but become worse. With reduced volumes of output of military goods, enterprises have been attempting to cover their overheads by charging higher prices for their civil products.

Notwithstanding the problems of the 1988 transfers, the policy of switching capacity from the civilian sector to the defence industry was taken a stage further in the following year. As noted in Chapter 2, the government reorganization in the summer of 1989 changed the boundaries of the defence complex. The new Ministry of Atomic Energy and Industry took over a number of equipment-supply enterprises that were previously under civilian machinebuilding ministries. The reorganized Ministry of Communications took over some production capacity formerly outside the defence industry, and a number of enterprises manufacturing computers were removed from the civilian sector. In addition, almost the entire medical equipment industry was absorbed into the defence complex, the new lead organization being the Ministry of General Machinebuilding.[7] As a consequence of these changes, the defence complex has expanded in terms of facilities and personnel and now finds itself with a decisive role in meeting pressing consumer and welfare needs. As might be expected, it has been under mounting political pressure to achieve quick results. Also not surprising is the fact that this transfer policy does not enjoy wholehearted support from either within or outside the defence sector.

The policy of defence-sector reorientation has involved efforts to promote more substantial technology transfer from military to civilian activities. As the author has documented elsewhere, this is not a new policy, but it is now being given an additional impetus, facilitated by the declassification of hitherto secret facilities and technologies.[8] Until recently, much faith was placed in cross-sectoral diffusion through the provision of scientific and technical information, a prominent role being played by the Institute of Inter-branch Information (VIMI), which has been concerned both with the acquistion and processing of information on militarily useful foreign technologies and with domestic transfers. In the past such transfers were largely unplanned and unmonitored. Now more attention is being devoted to mechanisms and procedures for more effective use of defence-sector technologies for civil purposes, to overcome what Gorbachev has on a number of occasions termed the 'internal COCOM' of the Soviet economy.

The new transfer policy began to emerge in 1989 and was at first associated with the declassification of materials and other technologies associated with the 'Buran' space-shuttle programme. Given that the space programme in general, and the shuttle project in particular, faced growing pressure for budget cuts, this starting-point is not surprising, and support for a transfer policy undoubtedly serves the current interests of the ministry most directly concerned: the Ministry of General Machinebuilding. To the forefront in transfer efforts have been previously secret facilities of this ministry, including the Kaliningrad NPO 'Komposit', an important centre for the creation of advanced materials, and the industry's lead organization for production technologies, the Moscow NPO

'Tekhnomash'.[9] Work has been undertaken on the elaboration of a pro-gramme for technology transfer covering more than twenty different fields.[10] It is intended that some 400 scientific and technical achievements of the military-space industry will find application in the civilian economy.[11] Declassified technologies are also being offered abroad, with prospects for the creation of joint ventures for their exploitation. An early example is an agreed joint venture linking an Italian company and two facilities of the Ministry of General Machinebuilding ('Komposit' and 'Avangard') for the development of food industry and other equipment based on composite materials.[12] In September 1990 a new company, Anglo–Soviet Materials, mounted a display of advanced materials in London, many having their origin in space and military programmes.

Conversion: in search of a strategy

The conclusion of the INF Treaty put the conversion of defence-industry facilities onto the policy agenda, and the Votkinsk machinebuilding plant in the Udmurt Autonomous Republic, responsible for the SS–20 and other missiles covered by the agreement, became the first practical example of an attempt to reprofile capacity.[13] With the announcement of unilateral force reductions at the end of 1989, conversion was quickly transformed into a policy matter of the highest priority.

A word that was new to the Russian language only three years ago, *konversiya* is now a term in everday use. In public discussion it tends to be employed very loosely to describe almost anything connected with reduced military expenditure, or any civil activity undertaken by the armed forces or the defence industry. But within Gosplan, the VPK and the defence complex itself it is used in a narrower, more strict sense to refer to the organization of civilian production or R&D on the basis of capacities and resources formerly devoted to military work. In some Soviet, and also Western, discussion, distinction is sometimes made between conversion and diversification – a distinction often accompa-nied by a value judgment, explicit or implicit, that from the point of view of demilitarization, or simply 'peace', conversion is good and diversifica-tion bad. In reality, such a distinction is difficult to sustain, and general-ized discussion as to the relative merits of the two approaches can quickly degenerate into an unproductive polarization of positions. Diversification is understood to be entry into new civil activities by firms engaged in military work while the basic military capability is retained intact, albeit at a lower level of activity. In practice, as Soviet experience testifies, diversification often involves at least partial conversion, in particular the reassignment of personnel – managerial, technical and shopfloor – formerly engaged in military work. Furthermore, the new civil activities may draw to some extent on production capacities previously used wholly or predominantly for defence work, such as foundries, forges, toolrooms and other specialized facilities. This is especially likely to occur in the conditions of Soviet industry in so far as the overall level of specialization is low: a typical Soviet engineering plant undertakes a wide range of activities in-house that in the West would be undertaken by external, specialized subcontractors.

In the past it has always been maintained by Soviet writers that conversion will be carried out more easily in their economy because of the advantages of social ownership and central planning. It is ironic, therefore, that efforts for practical conversion have coincided with economic reform that is designed to limit the scope of central planning and to promote enterprise autonomy and market relations. There is no doubt that the transition to self-financing in the defence industry from January 1989, and the adoption of other reform measures, including the creation of cooperatives and, more recently, joint stock companies, has complicated the conversion process. It has also made the planning of conversion a more controversial issue than would have been the case in the absence of economic reform. It soon became apparent that two different philosophies were in contention: a traditional, highly centralized approach based on administrative, top-down planning, and an alternative, decentralized, bottom-up approach claimed to be in the spirit of the economic reform.[14] In the event it was basically the traditional approach that was employed for the elaboration of the State Programme for Conversion of the Defence Industry and the Development of Civilian Production in the Defence Complex to 1995.

This basic planning document for conversion is largely a product of the Gosplan defence-industry department, overseen by First Deputy Chairman Smyslov, in consulation with the VPK and the Ministry of Defence.[15] Promised for the end of 1989, a draft was discussed by the Presidium of the Council of Ministers at the end of February 1990 and again a week later by the Committee for Questions of Defence and State Security of the USSR Supreme Soviet. Its delay provoked bitter criticism, including an extraordinary attack by Oleg Baklanov, then Central Committee secretary for the defence industry, on the competence of the Council of Ministers and, by implication, Prime Minister Nikolai Ryzhkov.[16] The draft conversion programme was sent back for reconsideration and did not emerge again until the end of September, when it was discussed by Gorbachev's Presidential Council.[17] Further changes were made, and eventually, more than a year late, the programme was approved for implementation by a decree of the USSR Council of Ministers in December 1990. Since its approval, however, not only has there been no supporting legislation to secure its implementation, but it has become apparent that many important issues remain unresolved.

One of the most controversial issues of conversion has been the question of priorities: which civilian goods are to have first claim on released capacity? From the outset, the party and government authorities, probably reflecting Gorbachev's personal view, consistently granted first priority to consumer-related products, above all to equipment for the food and light industries, consumer goods and medical equipment. Lower in priority were electronics, civil aircraft and shipbuilding. From early 1989, in accordance with these priorities and in the absence of an approved programme, conversion focused on consumer and welfare-related goods as enterprises attempted to adapt to reduced military orders. Enterprises found themselves under pressure from their ministries, local party organizations and soviets to rapidly organize the production of goods in short supply, often with little regard to the production possibilities of the enterprises concerned. Criticism of this policy led to some modification of priorities in the final version of the State Programme. Some fields of scientific and technical development that are considered especially important are covered by priority state programmes of union scope, including civil aviation, civil shipbuilding, space research for economic purposes, communications and a major conversion programme for the nuclear industry. Faced with both military cuts and the post-Chernobyl rundown of the civil nuclear-power programme, the nuclear industry is embarking on a programme of development of advanced materials, microelectronics, computer and fibre-optic communications technologies.

Other priority areas include technically complex consumer goods, equipment for the food and light industries, medical equipment, electronics and computing, and environmental control equipment.[18] The planned expansion of output of a range of civilian goods is shown in Table 4.1, which also provides an indication of the level of civil involvement of the defence complex in 1988, prior to the adoption of the conversion policy.

The overall scale of conversion is difficult to determine with accuracy, because Soviet sources rarely make a clear distinction between genuine conversion and the expansion of pre-exisiting civilian activities. According to the autumn 1990 draft State Programme, the civil share of the gross output of the defence complex is to increase from 43 per cent in 1989 to 50 per cent in 1990 and 65 per cent in 1995.[19] Between 1988 and 1995 the volume of civilian output is to more than double.[20] Intentions with regard to the growth of military output to 1995 are unclear, but the available evidence suggests that the aim is to maintain a stable level of annual output during the period 1991–5. Analysis of the known targets of the State Programme indicates that conversion as such will not be the principal factor in the envisaged increase in civil output during the period to 1995. More important will be the planned expansion of well-established civilian activities of the defence complex, coupled with additional output obtained from the capacities transferred to the complex during 1988–9.[21]

Another policy issue concerns the spread of conversion: should it be realized on a partial scale at many enterprises? Or should it be concentrated at a smaller number of facilities, wholly, or substantially, freed from military work? The evidence points to the adoption of the former. According to the draft State Programme, conversion will be undertaken at 428 enterprises of the defence complex and at a further 100 enterprises of other ministries. Of the former, 242 enterprises, or 56 per cent, will reduce their military work by 20 per cent or less, and only 6 will undergo full conversion to civil work, compared with 34 of the enterprises of other ministries.[22] One gains the impression that the defence-sector ministries are reluctant to see full conversion, involving permanent withdrawal of capacity from military production. Instead, they are preferring an 'equal-misery' approach, obliging many enterprises to combine military and civilian production, even though, as critics point out, the retention of military output, albeit at a reduced level, may not permit the genuine conversion of facilities to specialized civilian work. That the official

Table 4.1 The non-military production of the defence complex

Product	1988	1990	1995 forecast†
Steel (m.tonnes)	14	11	—
% total	9	7	—
Civil aircraft (b.r.)	—	1.3	2.7
% total	—	100	100
Civil ships (b.r.)	—	1.2	1.8
% total	—	<100	<100
Passenger cars (t.u.)	—	132	—
% total	—	11	—
Motorcycles & scooters (t.u.)	601	540	740
% total	56	53	—
Bicycles (t.u.)	2461	2488	3400
% total	44	43	—
Tractors (t.u.)	83	67	—
% total	15	14	—
NC machine tools (t.u.)	4.5	3.2	—
% total	20	14	—
Food industry equipment (m.r.)	1033	1672	3800
% total	78	80	82
Light industry equipment (m.r.)	—	—	2430
% total	—	—	90
Trade & public catering equipment (m.r.)	—	—	1250
% total	—	—	89
Medical equipment (m.r.)	210	1280	3060
% total	19	80	87
Communications equipment (b.r.)	—	1.8	3.7
% total	<100	100	100
Television sets (t.u.)	9637	10500	15000
% total	100	100	100

Table 4.1 (*continued*)

Product	1988	1990	1995 forecast†
Video recorders (t.u.)	73	454	2400
% total	100	100	100
Tape recorders (t.u.)	5406	6175	7500
% total	<100	98	<100
Refrigerators/freezers (t.u.)	6089	6025	8700
% total	98	93	—
Washing-machines (t.u.)	4420*	5215	7700
% total	66*	66	—
Vacuum cleaners (t.u.)	3722	4025	6700
% total	78	69	—
Sewing-machines (t.u.)	1550	1753	3200
% total	100	100	100
Cameras (t.u.)	2722	3079	4000
% total	100	100	100
Clocks and watches (m.u.)	16	17*	—
% total	22	23*	—
Furniture (m.r.)	—	405	579
% total	—	4	—
All consumer goods (b.r.)	26.6	38.3	71.0
% total	12	15	—

*1989
†Targets of the State Programme for Conversion. The forecast percentages of total output take no account of possible new production by the non-state sector of industry.
t. – thousand; m. – million; b. – billion; u. – units; r. – roubles; the absence of a figure indicates that no data are available.
Source: Compiled from numerous Soviet publications.

approach to conversion is one designed to keep open the option of increased military production in case of necessity has been confirmed by one of the authors of the State Programme, V. Kotov. Enterprises cannot be fully converted and effectively removed from the defence industry, he maintains, because all defence enterprises must retain secret 'regime' facilities.[23] This policy probably reflects successful lobbying by the military, whose traditional thinking on military preparedness, with few exceptions, will not allow conversion to be irreversible.

For decades, public discussion of policy for the military preparedness of the Soviet economy was strictly forbidden. It was only in the autumn of 1990 that critics of the thinking behind the State Programme were able to bring the issue out into the open. In putting forward an alternative conception of conversion, the economists Yu. A. Yaremenko and E. A. Rogovskii called for a review of mobilization policy permitting a release of the reserve capacities maintained at great expense in many branches of industry.[24] When the State Programme was adopted in December 1990, it was decided that further research would be undertaken into the question of preparedness for mobilization, and in April 1991 the issue was discussed for the first time by the Supreme Soviet's Committee on Questions of Defence and State Security.[25] At this meeting, held in camera, the military are reported to have defended vigorously their traditional ideas, refusing to consider a change of policy. One reason for this intransigence appears to be that those responsible for mobilization policy are hopelessly ill-informed on the policies of Western countries, grotesquely exaggerated assessments of the potential for mobilization of the US defence industry having wide currency. In the words of a critic – Vitalii Shlykov, deputy chairman of the Russian republic's Committee for Questions of Defence – the present system of mobilization preparedness is a 'holy cow', which the central, union, structures of power strive to defend at all costs.[26] Shlykov and other critics charge that Soviet official thinking on economic preparedness for war has not changed since the 1930s, and maintain that a change of policy would permit the release of substantial, 'dead' production capacity throughout the economy, while also allowing more radical conversion of enterprises of the defence industry.

Any expectation that conversion could provide a means of enhancing civilian capabilities with a minimum of investment quickly evaporated.

Very soon after the adoption of the policy, leading representatives of both the defence industry and the armed forces began to argue that conversion would be a costly process requiring substantial additional capital outlays. Indeed, this became such a constant refrain that one suspects its deliberate use as a means of exerting pressure on the authorities to moderate the conversion drive. The draft State Programme to 1995 provides for budget-funded investment in the civilian activities of the defence complex of 41.5 billion roubles, of which 9 billion roubles will be used for the reprofiling of military-related capacities, and 30 billion roubles for the creation of new capacities for civilian production. Some of the funding will finance the conservation of military production facilities that have been withdrawn from active use. The evidence suggests that the incidence of conversion-related investment will be especially heavy in the initial period, from 1990 to 1992. It is difficult to see how this ambitious investment programme can be sustained given the substantial state budget deficit. On the other hand, there will be savings from reduced levels of investment for military production. The plan for 1990 provided for centralized state investment in the defence complex of half the level originally foreseen in the five-year plan, and it is claimed that construction work on 300 new defence enterprises has been halted. Some of the projects may be completed as civilian facilities.[27]

According to the draft State Programme, in 1990 alone 500,000 workers were to leave employment in military production and transfer to civilian work. Budget funds are being allocated to cover the cost of retraining displaced workers and to provide some protection of levels of earnings. Between 1989 and 1992, total budget allocations for retraining and for compensation for loss of pay are planned to reach almost 1 billion roubles.[28] A more substantial burden to the budget has been the maintenance of enterprise funds for bonuses, social measures and the development of production. These funds are normally created from retained profits, but, with military cuts and conversion, enterprise profitability has declined sharply; indeed, many defence-sector plants are now operating at a loss. According to Baklanov, during 1989 and 1990, state-budget finance of 6 billion roubles was allocated to maintain enterprise funds.[29] At the same time, budget revenue from the defence complex has declined because enterprises undergoing conversion are being given lower targets for payments into the budget from profits.[30] There is no doubt that

41

conversion is now imposing a considerable burden on an overstrained state budget, absorbing a considerable proportion of savings from reduced outlays on defence.

An extremely contentious aspect of conversion policy is the reduced level of funding for military R&D and the partial switch of defence-related research and design facilities to civilian work. As part of the original unilateral cuts announced at the end of 1989, it was envisaged that R&D funded by the Ministry of Defence budget would be reduced by 15 per cent during 1989–91.[31] In 1990, R&D funding was reduced to 13.2 billion roubles, compared with 15.3 billion roubles in 1989, a 14 per cent reduction, suggesting that most of the envisaged cuts had been undertaken. However, as noted in Chapter 1, further substantial cuts were made in the 1991 military budget. Prominent representatives of the armed forces have not concealed their anxiety about the scale of these R&D cuts, arguing that, in the absence of equivalent reductions in the United States and other NATO member countries, they are endangering the country's national security. They also point out, not without justice, that the reductions run counter to the officially declared policy of enhancing security through a qualitative improvement of Soviet military hardware. Within the defence industry some of the R&D conversion now under way has provoked outspoken opposition, above all from leading representatives of the aviation industry, who have campaigned with vigour against what they consider an inappropriate use of the industry's research and design skills.[32]

According to the draft State Programme, the partial reorientation of the research system of the defence complex will raise the civil share of performed R&D from 28.5 per cent in 1988 to almost 45 per cent in 1995. The priority civil-research field will be information technology: 1995 R&D expenditure will be 3.7 times the level of 1990. During 1991–5 state-budget funding of civil R&D undertaken by the defence complex will amount to 36 billion roubles.[33] However, it is apparent that conversion as such will make a relatively modest contribution. From the draft State Programme it can be estimated that in 1995 'conversion' R&D will represent less than 10 per cent of total R&D performed by the defence complex, but almost one-fifth of its civilian component.

Practical problems

Since the adoption of the conversion policy, many enterprises and R&D organizations have been faced with the need to cope with reduced military orders. Undoubtedly, there has been much 'pseudo conversion' – the expansion of civilian output, often well established at the enterprises concerned, with little or no actual reprofiling of production capacities. But it would be wrong to classify all conversion to date as purely cosmetic. The Votkinsk works is by no means alone in undertaking a genuine transformation of production facilities previously devoted to military work. Many difficulties have appeared, partly stemming from the unplanned and haphazard way in which conversion has proceeded. It has been common for enterprises to be informed of substantial reductions in military orders without any prior warning, complicating the organization of alternative production.

A major problem has been the impact of conversion on the financial viability of enterprises. The value added during one hour of work on military products tends to be substantially higher than equivalent work on civilian goods, with negative consequences for enterprise profitability and the earnings of the labour force. Since reduced military orders usually relate to older types of equipment, which have been in production for many years and have high profit margins, even modest cutbacks can almost entirely eliminate enterprise profits and, as a result, can render the enterprise unable to create funds for incentives and social development. The maintenance of the latter is considered essential in order to retain skilled personnel.

There is no doubt that during the past two to three years many employees of the defence industry have experienced a deterioration in their pay in relation to other groups of workers. No longer is the defence complex a uniquely privileged sector of the economy in terms of financial reward and conditions of employment. To make matters worse, those working at enterprises in towns and regions with heavy concentrations of military production have often found that supplies of food and consumer goods have diminished sharply. In the past they were ensured privileged supply, but now the traditional administered supply system has broken down. The communist party has lost its ability to mobilize resources, and the defence-sector enterprises often lack civilian goods suitable for barter in exchange for supplies of food and consumer goods. As the general economic situation has deteriorated, the latter consideration has become a factor promoting conversion: enterprises have a direct interest in quickly organizing the manufacture of barterable goods, in particular high-value consumer items. The breakdown in traditional relations of supply has been felt with particular force by those living in the closed towns, who were formerly secured relatively comfortable conditions in exchange for some curtailment of civil liberties.

Loss of privilege, coupled with uncertainty as to future career prospects, has prompted workers and specialists to leave the defence industry in search of alternative employment. This applies in particular to younger, highly skilled personnel, who have been joining cooperatives, small enterprises and other new ventures of the burgeoning non-state sector of the economy. In some localities heavily dependent on military production and having limited possibilities for alternative civil employment, problems of unemployment have arisen. One of the first such cases concerned the town of Glazov in the Udmurt (autonomous) republic. The major employer is the Chepetsk mechanical works of the nuclear industry. Cuts in output led to redundancies, forcing the local authorities to organize an employment exchange, which has since been cited as a model for other regions.[34] In other cases unemployment has been avoided by resort to short-time working and by granting employees exceptionally long holidays. At the beginning of July 1991, the new Soviet employment law came into force, providing for registration of the unemployed and payment of benefit. It is possible that managers of some defence-industry enterprises, previously inhibited from making employees redundant, will now take the opportunity to dismiss personnel freed by reduced military orders.

Faced with these practical problems, enterprise directors and the trade unions have been calling for action, in particular the adoption of a Law on Conversion that will provide a legal framework to ensure that conversion causes no deterioration of conditions of employment. The need for a law has been officially acknowledged for almost two years, and draft proposals have been submitted by interested organizations. The matter has been considered by the Supreme Soviet Committee for Questions of Defence and State Security, which in October 1990 discussed a draft prepared by the VPK, but without a definite outcome.[35] A law was promised for the session of the Supreme Soviet during the first half of

1991, but no progress appears to have been made. In recent months there has been clear evidence of prevarication on the part of the USSR government. Pavlov, the prime minister, argued, no doubt correctly, that many in the defence industry had exaggerated expectations of the potential of a Law on Conversion, and sought to present this state of affairs as grounds for delay.[36] Anatolii Luk'yanov, chairman of the USSR Supreme Soviet, echoed this view, further arguing that a fully elaborated programme for conversion should precede the adoption of a law.[37] The real issue of contention is probably the scale of compensation for losses incurred as a result of military cuts and conversion; the defence industry may well be insisting on a degree of protection that the government is unwilling to concede at a time of severe budget deficit. Meanwhile, in the absence of a Law on Conversion, the Council of Ministers in August 1990 adopted a decree providing for some limited protection of the pay and conditions of workers at enterprises undergoing conversion.[38]

The problems and uncertainties of conversion have generated doubts, tension and opposition. In Leningrad by the autumn of 1989, it had become popularly known as *konvulsiya!*[39] Rarely does one find open opposition to the principle of conversion, rather it is the manner in which it is being undertaken that is arousing hostility, with evidence that many defence-sector personnel consider the present policy and its implementation to be incompetent and damaging to their interests. Factory managers frequently observe that their enterprises have 'fallen under conversion' in the same way as one might speak of falling under a bus. Critical comment on conversion became a regular feature of party gatherings, from the Central Committee to local meetings, and also of sessions of the USSR and republican parliaments. As discussed in the next chapter, one sign of discontent has been the open advocacy of a more vigorous arms export policy, seen by some as a means of avoiding, or mitigating, conversion. For many, both within and outside the defence industry, the over-riding concern is that the unique research and manufacturing capabilities of the military sector, built up over many years, are being rapidly erroded, threatening not only the future military capability of the country but also its potential for economic revival.

A striking feature of the Soviet conversion effort has become the extent to which, in the absence of an authoritative national programme, enterprises have been seeking their own solutions, often by entering into collaborative projects at a local or regional level, or by establishing joint ventures with foreign companies. This is one of the most optimistic and positive aspects of the process, offering some prospect that worthwhile results will be achieved. Cities and regions with active local conversion programmes involving inter-ministerial associations and consortia include Moscow, Leningrad, Novosibirsk, Kiev, Kazan, Perm' and Sverdlovsk. In the Urals, the local 'Uralkonversiya' association began by bringing together enterprises faced with reduced military orders, but then it was decided that a more commercial approach was required. Conversion is now a central concern of 'Bol'shoi Ural', a joint stock corporation established in October 1990.[40] The Udmurt republic has elaborated a territorial conversion programme for local enterprises hard hit by military cuts, and a similar initiative is being promoted in the Far East.[41] In some case the associations have set up commercial banks to finance civil projects. The local concerns and associations are also playing an increasingly important role in promoting contacts with foreign companies. These grass-roots initiatives are stimulating interest in the possibilities offered to defence-sector enterprises by market reform and are leading to a growing impatience with the petty tutelage exercised by the ministries in Moscow. They are also serving to strengthen within the defence complex itself hostility to the thinking behind the State Programme. In the words of Valentin Zanin, general director of the Leningrad 'Signal' association, the 'gigantic, all-embracing scheme of conversion' of Gosplan 'in no way differs from the Food Programme of sorry repute' and as such represents a variant of the 'dead-end administrative system of managing production'.[42] What is now developing is a form of entrepreneurial conversion from below, increasingly calling into question the traditional administrative thinking of the centre and, at the same time, boosting the constituency in favour of market reform.

From conversion to demilitarization?
There is no disagreement between Gorbachev and more radical reformers that the Soviet Union has an excessively militarized economy. Over the past two years there has been growing support for the view that what is required is not simply partial conversion of the defence industry as set out in the State Programme, but a decisive demilitarization of the economy.

This position has been argued forcefully by many academic specialists and has found more concrete embodiment in an alternative conception of conversion advanced by a research group headed by Yurii A. Yaremenko, director of the Institute for National Economic Forecasting of the USSR Academy of Sciences. In 1990 Yaremenko, a corresponding member of the Academy, was elected to the Communist Party Central Committee.

Yaremenko first put forward his proposals for conversion in a report submitted to the Council of Ministers in August 1990.[43] The point of departure of his alternative conception is a conviction that the structure of the Soviet economy is so highly distorted that it will be extremely difficult to make a successful transition to a market economy. Indeed, in a polemical intervention in *Pravda* at the beginning of September 1990, Yaremenko expressed his belief that, without radical structural change, transition to market prices would lead to the collapse 'of the entire totality of economic relations ... like a house of cards'.[44] Far-reaching structural transformations are therefore required as a matter of urgency, in particular a decisive reduction in the share of the military sector and a rapid development of the sphere related to consumption. Price distortions conceal the true magnitude of the military sector and the degree of structural deformation of the economy. According to estimates contributed by Rogovskii, the share of weapons and other military hardware in the combined final output of the defence and machinebuilding complexes is 62 per cent when calculated in world prices, compared with 31 per cent when expressed in Soviet current price terms. What is required, it is argued, is determined action to reduce the size of the military sector to the minimum scale necessary to meet the country's genuine security needs in the new international climate. All facilities not vital to this core armaments industry should be removed from the defence complex and transformed whenever possible into autonomous joint stock companies. Such converted firms would become poles of high technology, facilitating the restructuring and modernization of the civilian economy. They would also establish links with foreign companies and seek to export high-grade manufactured goods. At the same time, it is argued, the traditional Soviet approach to the maintenance of spare mobilization capacity, identified as a major source of inefficiency, has to be completely revised.

This alternative strategy for conversion immediately attracted attention, since it was incorporated wholesale into Stanislav Shatalin's '500 days' programme for transition to a market economy. Some elements also appeared in the later 'Basic Directions' economic programme adopted by the USSR Supreme Soviet in October 1990. In the latter programme, conversion was placed much more centrally than ever before in the context of overall economic restructuring, and it was also hinted that enterprises not essential to military production would be permitted to leave the union ministries of the defence complex.[45] Later, when the State Programme for conversion was approved in December, it was indicated that the Yaremenko team would continue its work, examining more radical conversion scenarios.

Developments in 1991 indicate that policy for conversion remains an open issue. At a meeting of economists in March, Gorbachev observed that no one was satisfied with the conversion programme and noted his intention to return to the matter. On this occasion he also made explicit his agreement with Yaremenko on the urgent need for more radical structural change.[46] Two months later, Yaremenko was appointed a part-time adviser to the president.[47] In April, in a speech made en route to Japan, Gorbachev indicated that he was now thinking more in terms of an export-orientated policy for the defence industry, including, at least in the short term, exports of military hardware.[48] The view that the defence industry, in cooperation with Western partners, should spearhead an export drive in high technology goods has gained increasing support as conversion has developed.[49] In Japan, Gorbachev revealed that work was underway on a third, 'more mature', variant of the conversion programme. At the same time he reiterated his overall understanding: 'Today the defence sector is a definite burden for us. But it is also our enormous reserve.'[50]

There are evidently conflicting pressures at work. On the one hand, it is recognized widely that the economy is excessively militarized and that economic revival would be facilitated by a more radical transfer of capacities and skills to civil purposes. The urgent need to curb the state budget deficit is adding to pressure for a further reduction of military expenditure, a measure also being advocated by leaders of Western countries. On the other hand, within the defence complex there are major problems arising from the cuts implemented so far, giving rise to a widely held view that for the time being the industry has reached the limit of its ability to absorb reductions in military orders. An expression of this is a growing fear of unemployment, a concern apparently shared by Pavlov, who in June declared that: 'Large-scale conversion threatens mass unemployment, which we will not be able to sustain.'[51] As indicated above, conversion is also proving to be extremely costly, requiring substantial budget outlays on investment and compensation for lost earnings of enterprises and personnel. In the words of Luk'yanov, speaking in July, 'The programme of conversion has turned out to be too expensive ... therefore the programme is now being reconsidered.'[52]

The possibility that the conversion effort could be moderated in response to short-term problems and conservatism in government and military circles has diminished following the failed coup attempt. With the dismissal of Pavlov, Yazov, Baklanov and other military and industrial leaders of conservative orientation, demilitarization is likely to be pursued with renewed vigour. Conversion can be expected to be based more firmly than ever on market principles. The likely scenario is one according to which enterprises freed substantially or wholly from military orders will be encouraged to convert into joint stock companies. They will be expected to raise their own finance to launch new civil production, possibly in partnership with Western firms, and to solve for themselves problems of personnel, pay and conditions. Republican governments are likely to play a much larger role in shaping conversion policy. At the union level, any remaining state support can be expected to be confined to a very limited number of major programmes identified as being of genuine national importance.

The reorientation of the Soviet defence industry has made significant progress during the past three years, despite countless difficulties and obstacles. It is still too early to expect substantial results, although in some specific fields – such as the development and manufacture of medical equipment and some consumer goods – there are already real achievements. Less satisfactory has been the involvement of the defence complex in the production of equipment for the food and consumer industries, mainly because a serious mistake was made in spreading the work widely among many enterprises entirely lacking experience. Progress can be seen in the nuclear and aviation industries, but difficulties are much more acute, and achievements less, in the Ministry of the Defence Industry with its plants producing tanks, artillery and munitions. In general it appears to be towns and regions dominated by facilities of this ministry, for example Tula and Nizhnii Tagil, that are experiencing the most severe problems, suggesting that in this more traditional industry there is a lack of entrepreneurial initiative. This mixed outcome is only to be expected. Much depends now on the extent to which the defence industry can maintain the process of transformation in circumstances of severe economic dislocation, break-up of the union, and moves in the direction of a market economy.

5

THE DEFENCE INDUSTRY AND ECONOMIC REFORM

It is not surprising that radical economic reform is a sensitive issue for the Soviet defence industry. After all, it represents the core of the traditional administrative system and is its principal beneficiary. The strength and position of the defence complex is such that it is able to exert strong influence on policy for reform. There is no doubt that not all administrators and managers of the complex show enthusiasm for the goal of a mixed, market economy. However, scepticism or outright opposition are not the only responses: within the defence industry more positive positions can be found. Again, this should not be a matter for surprise. The military sector possesses some of the best technical and managerial talents present in the Soviet economy, precisely those personnel best-equipped in terms of skills, if not always of attitude, to respond to the challenges of a market economy. It is also the only sector of the economy with long experience of external competitive pressure.

Until recent changes, the Soviet defence industry epitomized the administrative-command system. All facilities were state-owned. Enterprises were subject to detailed central planning with overall coordination realized by the VPK. Supplies of equipment and materials were guaranteed through the administered state-supply system, which granted the defence complex priority in terms of both quantity and, above all, quality. Prices of all inputs and of the end-product weapons were centrally fixed, the entire price system being biased in such a way as to keep down the cost of military hardware supplied to the armed forces. Those working in the defence complex were accustomed to obtaining generous state-budget funding for military R&D, for investment in new facilities and for underwriting costly military projects through hidden subsidies. The privileged financial and pricing arrangements had the effect of making a rouble in the defence industry worth considerably more than a rouble in the civil economy; 'gold' roubles instead of the usual 'wooden', to use terms often employed by Soviet writers.

At the enterprise level there were not only special success indicators and bonuses for rewarding full compliance with contractual obligations and measures for cost reduction, but also unusually strict procedures for ensuring high-quality output, with direct involvement of the military customer. Those working in the defence industry were used to relatively high levels of financial reward and access to above-average housing, welfare and leisure provision. Characteristic of this privileged enclave of the economy was an extraordinarily ramified system of secrecy going far beyond the requirements of military security. Although this system was highly restrictive and must have caused great inconvenience to those working within the defence complex, for the ministries and organizations it had a positive side: disasters, incompetence and waste could be concealed from external scrutiny, and it helped to shield privileges and perks from the critical and envious appraisal of those beyond the enclave's boundaries. The 'closed' zones and towns became the ultimate expression of this philosophy. Of vital importance to the functioning and maintenance of this system of priority and secrecy were the communist party and the KGB; in no other part of the economy did they exert such all-pervasive influence.

Given the economic arrangements hitherto characteristic of the defence industry, it is not surprising that the Soviet authorities were initially cautious in seeking to develop within it the new institutions and principles of market reform. In the absence of military cuts, conversion and general economic disintegration, it is likely that the defence sector would have been isolated to a substantial degree from radical reform initiatives. In the event, the military sector has increasingly found itself pushed and pulled into the mainstream of the transition process leading to a market economy. Like its civil counterpart, it is now coming to terms with issues of ownership, market institutions and republican economic sovereignty.

Turning to the market

Of all the ministries of the defence complex it was the aviation industry that was first to consider new economic arrangements and forms of ownership. Minaviaprom has a well-established economic research institute in Moscow, the Research Institute for Economics, Planning and Management, under the directorship of Aleksandr Isaev. Isaev and his colleagues caused a stir in 1989 when they put forward a proposal for a new form of 'collective' ownership as an alternative to the all-pervasive state ownership found in Soviet industry. Enterprises would become the property of those who worked at them, or ownership would be shared between the state and the workforce.[1]

In 1990 there were attempts to put the new approach into practice at the Saratov aviation works, the producer of the Yak–42 airliner. This enterprise has experienced severe economic difficulties because the price of the aircraft was fixed at far too low a level for profitable operation. A scheme was elaborated to convert the works into a collectively owned enterprise in the hope that this would secure viable operation. However, although he initially gave his support, the minister, A. S. Systsov, blocked the plan, much to the chagrin of Isaev and the enterprise's director, A. Ermishin.[2]

In the autumn of 1990, the Isaev team put forward its own programme for transition to a market economy as an alternative to both the government's strategy and Shatalin's '500 days' scenario. At the heart of the so-called '*Paritet*' ('Parity') programme was a scheme for the transformation of state property into collectively owned assets by means of widescale free transfers of shares to enterprise employees, i.e. the generalization of the approach proposed originally for the aircraft industry alone. The 'Parity' programme received some sympathetic support, but never achieved the status of a major reform option on a par with the Shatalin '500 days' programme.[3]

The boldness of Isaev and his colleagues has paid off. Ministerial opposition has been overcome. Two of the ministry's associations in Saratov – the aircraft factory and the electrical equipment works, the products of which include the 'Saratov' domestic refrigerator, one of the country's best models – have begun the transition to a non-state form of ownership. The go-ahead was given by a decree of the USSR Council of Ministers. The radical economic paper *Kommersant* has described them as the first privatized enterprises of the Soviet defence industry.[4] At the beginning of 1991, 40–50 per cent of the assets of each association were transferred free of charge to their work collectives. The remaining assets, at their written-down value, are to be bought out over a period from enterprise earnings. The enterprises are now considered to be fully owned by their work collectives, which can dispose of the assets as they choose. This is strictly an employee share ownership scheme: shares are not tradable outside the enterprises. It has been suggested that this method of transforming state-owned enterprises may have especially wide application in the defence sector, since the value of their productive funds are effectively halved at a stroke, facilitating profitable operation from the outset. However, experience has quickly shown that the new form of ownership is not without problems.

For the Saratov aviation factory the first few months of work in conditions of collective ownership have not been easy. The new company decided to put up the price of the Yak–42, but Aeroflot, effectively a monopoly purchaser on the domestic market, immediately responded by refusing to buy the Saratov-built plane. The company is now attempting to secure more foreign customers, meanwhile operating on bank credit.[5] At the electrical equipment company the workers, the new 'owners', threatened to strike in protest against inadequate compensation for higher retail prices. As a critic of the form of privatization adopted at Saratov has pointed out, the very fact that the 'owners' can contemplate striking against themselves demonstrates the formal nature of the transfer of ownership from the state: a share-purchase scheme is likely to foster a more fundamental change of attitude.[6]

Since the pioneering move at Saratov, other defence-sector enterprises have taken initiatives to adopt new forms of ownership. Perhaps the most striking case is that of the vast 'Kirov factory' association in Leningrad, hard hit by reduced military orders and conversion. Developments here have great symbolic importance: the Putilov works was one of the foremost bastions of the Petrograd proletariat, its workers playing a prominent role in the revolutionary events of 1917 and in the early years of the Soviet regime. Having ceased tank production, the workforce, with encouragement from the radical city authorities of Leningrad, decided to transform the plant into a joint stock company and succeeded in obtaining the backing of the USSR Cabinet of Ministers. During the initial period the state will retain a holding of at least 50 per cent, the remaining shares being offered for sale to the workforce and also to outsiders, with the possibility of foreign participation.[7] It is likely that other Leningrad defence-complex enterprises, including the 'Svetlana' association of the electronics industry, will soon follow the Kirov factory's example, contributing to the city's project for the formation of a special economic region.

Willingness to develop new forms of ownership can also be found in the defence complex at enterprises concerned with consumer goods production. A good example is one of the famous plants of Soviet industry, the pre-Revolutionary 'Singer' sewing-machine factory at Podol'sk. In 1988 the PO 'Podol'skshveimash', the country's monopoly manufacturer of domestic sewing-machines, was taken over by the Ministry of the Defence Industry. At the beginning of 1991 it was converted into the joint stock concern 'Podol'sk', with capital assets leased from the ministry. In an attempt to demonopolize production within the concern, a number of independent production units have been organized. At the same time in Moscow, a firm called 'Optima' is being founded for marketing sewing-machines. This will include a number of small enterprises involved in the manufacture of clothing and footwear.[8]

An option now open to organizations of the defence sector is the co-founding of new joint stock companies. A good example is the Kiev-based joint stock company 'Perkom', shares in which went on sale in September 1990. Organized for activities in the field of information technology and in particular the production of personal computers, 'Perkom' has been founded by more than twenty enterprises and institutes of the electronics and radio industries, most of which are located in the Ukraine, together with organizations of the Ukrainian Academy of Sciences.[9]

So far, privatization within the defence complex has concerned enterprises engaged wholly or predominantly in civilian work. It still remains open whether non-state ownership will be permitted for enterprises with substantial involvement in military production. Although not ruling out such a development sometime in the future, the former prime minister, Pavlov, indicated that he was opposed to such a move in the short term.[10] The law on the basic principles of denationalization and privatization of enterprises adopted by the USSR Supreme Soviet in July 1991 certainly

permits the privatization of defence-complex enterprises of civil orientation. It is forecast that by the end of 1995 the proportion of state
ownership in the defence complex will be between 30 and 50 per cent of
the value of its capital stock.[11] This suggests that Pavlov's position has
been adopted: enterprises important for military production will remain
in the hands of the state. How long this position can be maintained is not
clear. The economist Vasilii Selyunin is not alone in thinking that
privatization is highly appropriate for enterprises of the defence sector. It
is argued that it will force them to compete for military orders or to
undertake conversion to profitable civil goods if such orders are not
obtainable.[12] Furthermore, if denationalization is successfully carried out
at some leading defence-sector enterprises of civil orientation, pressure
for privatization could arise from within the remaining state sector as
enterprises see the benefits of freedom from state control.

The defence industry has also been involved in the adoption of other
forms of non-state ownership. Enterprises and R&D organizations have
sponsored the formation of many cooperatives and small-scale, private
enterprises. Allowing enterprising personnel to form their own firms can
bring benefits to the parent organization. Operating under less restrictive
legislation, the cooperative or small enterprise can engage more freely in
commercial activity, make contacts with foreign companies, and in
general serve as a convenient 'front' for the state enterprise or institute.
They can also provide a means of evading the strict regulations on pay
that are characteristic of the defence sector, providing a means of offering
larger financial rewards to young, talented personnel. In the Ministry of
the Defence Industry alone there are more than 480 cooperatives attached
to enterprises. According to the former minister, Boris Belousov, many
have been created to overcome specific bottlenecks, and, although rates
of pay are double those of state enterprises, labour productivity is much
lower.[13] Among the founders of the new Association of Small Innovation
Enterprises, formed in the summer of 1991, was the state VPK, thereby
putting an official seal of approval on the formation of such firms within
the defence complex.

The enterprising aviation industry was one of the first ministries to
create a commercial bank to promote its own consumer goods production
and other civil activities. 'Aviabank' has been founded by a number of
enterprises of the industry, the insurance organization Ingosstrakh and

the USSR Agro-industrial Bank. Its foundation capital is modest at 130 million roubles.[14] Now many of the new commercial banks that have sprung up all over the country during the past two years have individual enterprises and institutes of the defence industry as co-founders.

One of the most striking manifestations of growing interest in market institutions on the part of enterprises of the defence complex has been their involvement in the establishment and operation of commodity exchanges. With the disintegration of the traditional system of central planning and supply, enterprises in Soviet industry have been forced to find alternative means of obtaining supplies of materials, fuel and equipment. In the absence of developed market relations and free market pricing, a network of commodity exchanges (*birzhy*), effectively auctions for industrial supplies and consumer goods, has developed with extraordinary rapidity since the Moscow Commodity Exchange was first registered in May 1990. By the summer of 1991, some 200 commodity exchanges, sometimes combined with stock exchanges, had been founded, the initiative often being taken by large enterprises or local commercial centres of the state supply organization. From the point of view of prospects for market reform, a significant feature of the mushrooming of exchanges is that they are usually founded by local entrepreneurial initiative, owing little if anything to central decisions from above. Indeed, so spontaneous and rapid has been their development that at the time of writing there is still no union legislation regulating their activities.

At first, enterprises of the defence industry appeared to have adopted a wary attitude to the new commodity exchanges, but this soon began to change. In so far as the system of administered supply of resources remained intact, the defence industry was the principal beneficiary; its enterprises may have had less reason than their civilian counterparts to resort to alternative sources of supply, at least for their basic military work. But, with conversion and expanded civilian involvement, even formerly protected defence-complex producers have increasingly encountered supply difficulties. Furthermore, they have felt the need to acquire additional supplies of food and consumer goods for their workers in an attempt to offset erosion of their pay and conditions.

A good example of defence sector involvement in the exchanges is the 'Udmurt republican commodity-stock universal exchange'. The founding shareholders of this exchange, established as a joint stock company in

57

April 1991, include most of the major associations of the defence industry located in Udmurtiya. It is envisaged that the exchange will not only provide a means of obtaining scarce resources, but that it will also organize exhibitions and sales of locally produced goods and promote contact with foreign firms. These activities should facilitate conversion.[15] Similar exchanges have been organized in such defence-industry centres as Sverdlovsk, Perm' and Novosibirsk. By the summer of 1991, commodity exchanges were beginning to appear in more remote towns: founders of the 'Angarskii region' exchange at Angarsk near Irkutsk include the local uranium enrichment plant and the nuclear industry's information institute, 'Atominform'.[16]

Once they had become involved in the founding of exchanges, it was a logical next step for organizations of the defence industry to establish their own 'Military-Industrial Exchange'. The initiative was taken jointly by leading facilities of the Ministry of General Machinebuilding – namely its Central Research Institute of Machinebuilding with its associated Space Flight Control Centre, both at Kaliningrad to the north of Moscow – and by the Russian Commodity and Raw Materials Exchange. The Flight Control Centre has allocated to the exchange spare facilities originally built for control of flights of the 'Buran' space shuttle, together with a dependable communications system permitting contact with defence enterprises and other commodity exchanges throughout the country. Only defence-complex enterprises can become shareholders of the exchange, which will have a special security department concerned with trade in items of a secret nature. The director of the Military-Industrial Exchange, S. P. Petrov, has expressed the view that it may become an institution engaged in the award of defence contracts on a competitive basis. In time it is also envisaged that the new exchange will establish links with commodity exchanges in other countries, while Kaliningrad will become the location of the headquarters of the National Congress of Exchanges.[17] In a separate initiative, many defence-industry enterprises have been involved in moves to set up an exchange specializing in electronics, radio and communications equipment.[18] To some extent the commodity exchanges are a surrogate for genuine market relations, but in the current chaotic circumstances they are providing an important new form of horizontal linkage between producers and customers, and as such represent a stepping stone to a real market economy.

The general thrust of recent developments is in the direction of a weakening of the power of the industrial ministries, including those of the defence complex. Their ability to impose their will on the enterprises under their subordination is being steadily eroded. One factor is the rapid development of local initiatives for conversion with the creation of consortia and other novel organizational forms, coupled with the availability of new, decentralized sources of finance for investment easily obtained from the network of commercial banks. It is increasingly possible for enterprises to enter into local joint projects, or joint ventures with foreign firms, and present the ministries with *faits accomplis*. The development of such market and quasi-market forms may eventually mean that the ministries will be able to exert control only over production of a clearly expressed military character, leaving the producers completely free to determine the nature of their civilian activities. Such an outcome appears even more likely if account is taken of another dimension of the current situation: the push for economic sovereignty on the part of most republics of the USSR.

Union or republican?

As economic reform has evolved, and republican and local strivings for greater autonomy have strengthened, the traditional union structures of industrial administration have come under increasing strain. For the defence industry, with its highly centralized administrative arrangements, this is a particularly sensitive issue. The ministries of the defence complex are union ministries, and until recently no one questioned the appropriateness of this form of organization. But conversion and the growing civilian involvement of many enterprises have begun to pose the issue of whether such centralization is any longer justified except for a core group of facilities involved to a substantial degree in weapons development and production.

The concern of the defence-industry ministries has been heightened by developments in the Russian republic. At the time when the republic's government was considering the implementation of its own variant of the '500 days' programme in the autumn of 1990, the Russian prime minister, Ivan Silaev, a former minister of the aviation industry, made clear his conviction that a larger number of the enterprises of the defence complex located in Russia should be removed from their ministries and made independent. He looked forward to the retention of a single Ministry of the Defence Industry for oversight of those remaining as weapons-producing enterprises of a much smaller defence complex.[19] In adopting this stance, Silaev was being guided by the Shatalin programme's recommendations for conversion.

Recognizing that the USSR defence-sector ministries would be reluctant to release enterprises from their control, the Russian authorities began to adopt a policy of inducement, offering favourable conditions, above all in terms of taxation, to those enterprises deciding to transfer to RSFSR jurisdiction. For 1991, the Russian government originally decided to impose a 38 per cent rate of taxation on profits for all enterprises located in the republic; those of union status would have to pay the standard union rate of 45 per cent. In addition, a less restrictive policy on wages was adopted.[20] Faced with economic difficulties of conversion, these changes must look quite attractive to enterprises of the defence complex.

One of the first cases of an enterprise of the defence sector electing to transfer from union to republican control involved one of the metallurgical plants of the aviation industry. At the beginning of 1990 the Verkhnesaldinsk association (Sverdlovsk region), one of the world's largest producers of titanium, concluded a leasing agreement with Minaviaprom. A year later the ministry refused to prolong this agreement; in response, a conference of the association's workforce decided to withdraw the plant from the union ministry and to transfer it to the jurisdiction of the state bodies of the Russian republic.[21] This radical move, motivated by the desire to end ministerial petty interference, was resisted by Minaviaprom, which took legal action to restore its control. In the summer of 1991, a compromise was reached: the association remains under the union ministry, but on a leasing basis with substantial independence.[22]

The issue of union subordination became more tense in early 1991. The formation of the Cabinet of Ministers under the new prime minister, Pavlov, provided an opportunity to review the central institutions of economic administration, including the question of the continued existence of union industrial ministries. Some in the defence industry became alarmed that even the ministries of the military complex could face liquidation, or at least the transfer of some of their enterprises to republican subordination. Serious concern was signalled by interventions in the press by directors of a number of associations and enterprises.[23] These directors argued that the retention of union ministries was absolutely essential for the successful work of the weapons industry, not the least because it provided some guarantee that the nationwide supply relations would be maintained. In the event, the new Cabinet of Ministers provided for the retention of the union ministries of the defence sector, although with some changes of personnel.

During 1991 the issue of union or republican control of the defence industry has become a major issue of contention, with strong pressure being exerted not only by the Russian authorities, but also increasingly by other republics. The new Cabinet of Ministers of the Ukraine, formed in May 1991, includes for the first time a minister for questions of the defence complex and conversion. The minister, Viktor I. Antonov, a Russian by birth, has made clear the republic's intention to take control of defence-industry facilities located on Ukrainian territory from the beginning of 1992.[24] The right of the union authorities to direct weapons production is not contested, but the republic intends to gain control over all other aspects of the work of the industry. The Ukrainian authorities are seeking to win over the leaders of enterprises and R&D organizations by blaming the centre for all the negative consequences of conversion, and by promising effective assistance once republican control has been achieved. It has also been claimed that the defence industry of the Ukraine is on the verge of bankruptcy, largely because the centre has set prices for end products that have not adequately allowed for wage increases and higher prices of material inputs.[25] With less publicity, there have been similar moves in Kazakhstan, while in Estonia most defence-industry enterprises are now effectively recognizing republican authority by paying taxes according to local law.[26]

These developments were reflected in the evolution of thinking on the new Union Treaty. The version of March 1991 made explicit provision for the retention of union responsibility for the leadership of defence enterprises and organizations in so far as they are concerned with the production of weapons and other military hardware, but the civil production of such facilities was defined as a matter for joint union and republican leadership.[27] In the June 1991 version, the organization and leadership of the development and production of military hardware was retained as a union responsibility, but the management of enterprises of the defence complex and also, significantly, the organization of the mobilization preparedness of the economy were now regarded as matters of joint union and republican concern.[28] Even before the attempted coup, the trend of development was unmistakeable: the sphere of competence of the union ministries of the defence industry was being progressively whittled away, preparing the ground for an eventual replacement of them by a single union agency for the coordination of weapons development and production.

New relations with the armed forces

The impact of economic reform is not restricted to the defence industry, but is also beginning to affect the armed forces and the relations between weapons producers and military customers. These changes are potentially far-reaching and, as they develop, could permit more radical economic changes within the defence complex itself.

The Soviet armed forces possess a sizeable network both of enterprises, most of which are engaged in the repair and maintenance of military hardware, and of research establishments, some engaged in weapons R&D. These have traditionally operated as budget-financed organizations that are not subject to market pressures. During the past two to three years, economic reform measures have begun to be applied within this military sector, and, as military expenditure cuts have bitten more deeply, some facilities have also been faced with partial conversion to civil purposes. In some respects there is a convergence of economic arrangements in industry and the armed forces. Enterprises of the Ministry of Defence are now becoming engaged in civilian work, manufacturing consumer goods and certain types of industrial and transport equipment. The civilian share of their output is set to rise from 27.6 per cent in 1989 to 38.2 per cent in 1995. In absolute terms, however, their consumer-goods output is very modest, amounting to no more than a planned 300 million roubles in 1991.[29]

It is now widely held by representatives of the Ministry of Defence and the individual services that the traditional system of funding weapons procurement has put the military at a disadvantage in relation to the weapons industry. This supply-dominated relationship is claimed to have led to the transfer to the forces of hardware that was not meeting customer requirements in terms of technology and quality. In the past, the military customers were not able to air their grievances in public; with glasnost, they have not concealed their discontent with poor-quality hardware, exemplified by some naval equipment and the new Tu–160 'Blackjack' long-range bomber. The latter was transferred to the air force in an unfinished state, requiring extensive debugging to convert into a viable operational system.[30] The military have also complained of the lack of genuine competition between suppliers of similar types of hardware. As a deputy chairman of the Committee for Questions of Defence and State Security, V. Ochirov, has observed, similar models of military helicopters are developed by the competing Mil and Kamov design organizations, but, instead of the military selecting the best for production, both are manufactured in parallel in order to keep factories in work. Ochirov is confident that the development of market relations would allow the armed forces to obtain better value for money.[31]

Discussion of comprehensive military reform has included consideration of a new system of contractual relations between arms suppliers and customers. In brief, the military customers would be allocated financial resources for weapons procurement and would then be able to enter into contractual relations with suppliers of their own choice, i.e. a system of the type normal in Western countries. A similar system would operate for weapons-related R&D undertaken by organizations of the defence industry. The military is convinced that transition to this new system would give them genuine customer power, securing the development and production of high-grade weapons fully appropriate to their requirements. There is also an expectation that it would generate a more cost-conscious approach on the part of the suppliers. Not surprisingly, the defence industry does not share the military's enthusiasm, since many producers and design organizations could face loss of orders and potential closure. In the autumn of 1990, strong support for a market-type system of procurement was voiced by the then commander-in-chief of the air force, Evgenii Shaposhnikov, who asserted that: 'In conditions of the market we will come to different, more businesslike and democratic relations.'[32] Later in the year, the new system of financing weapons acquisition was incorporated into the Ministry of Defence's draft programme of military reform.[33] Now that Shaposhnikov is Minister of Defence, it is likely that the change will soon be put into practice. It could have a major impact on the work of the defence industry, possibly helping the transition to market relations in the military sector. The accumulating evidence suggests that it is a mistake to conclude that the Soviet armed forces are opposed to market reform: as conditions change, some of its representatives are beginning to perceive that in relation to the arms producers their position could be enhanced.

Exports as an alternative?
Faced with military cuts and conversion, it is not surprising that some representatives of the defence industry have been tempted by an alternative policy of seeking to expand arms exports. This temptation has been strengthened by the development of economic reform. In the past, enterprises and design organizations had little direct interest in the promotion of exports, but now the liberalization of external economic relations is opening up new possibilities.

Until recently, Soviet arms exports were shrouded in almost total secrecy. The export of military equipment has been a tightly controlled state monopoly handled by the Ministry of Foreign Economic Relations in consultation with the Ministry of Defence and the Foreign Ministry, although this last appears to have played a secondary role. The defence-industry ministries do not appear to have had any major say. The scale of exports was first revealed early in 1991, when I. S. Belousov revealed that in 1990 military exports had amounted to approximately 9.7 billion roubles, and during the five years 1986–90, 56.7 billion roubles.[34] Their volume was thus quite substantial, representing one-sixth of total Soviet exports during the period.

According to the traditional arrangements for arms exports, proceeds from the sale of weapons for foreign currency, as opposed to barter deals or generous credit terms involving negligible or non-existent repayment, are paid into the state budget. The producers are paid in domestic roubles and normally have not received any of the hard currency earned. According to the chief designer of the 'MiG–29', M. Val'denberg, the design bureau concerned receives no direct allocation from profits earned from exports, while the ministry obtains a 'miserly percentage' share.[35] Reforms in the foreign trade system during recent years have changed the position of enterprises exporting civil goods. Not only can they trade directly with foreign partners, bypassing the central authorities, but they can also keep part of their foreign currency earnings and use them for imports of equipment or of consumer goods for their workers. It is not surprising that directors of enterprises involved in military production have been agitating for similar rights.

It is the aircraft industry that has been most prominent in campaigning for increased exports as a means of partially offsetting cuts and the requirement for conversion. One of the most vigorous advocates of such a policy has been Mikhail Simonov, general designer of the Sukhoi design bureau. This bureau used to work almost exclusively on military aircraft. Its military work has been cut sharply, and it has been forced rapidly to establish a civil aviation programme. A similar stance has also been adopted by the Mikoyan bureau under its leader, R. A. Belyakov. Their argument is very simple: it is much better to export high-technology fighters for up to 20 million dollars per plane and use the proceeds to import consumer and other civil goods, than to convert aircraft design and production facilities to the manufacture of civil products for which they are often quite unsuited. Given the shortage of hard currency and the limited possibilities for Soviet exports of manufactured goods, it is not surprising that efforts have been made to boost military aircraft exports. Over the past twelve months there have been efforts to sell 'Su' and 'MiG' military planes to a number of countries, including Finland, Switzerland and China. Following the Gulf war, efforts have also been made to promote export sales of the Soviet equivalent of the 'Patriot' anti-missile system, the 'S–300' developed by the radio industry's NPO 'Almaz', led by Academician Boris Bunkin.[36] It appears that design organizations and enterprises now have greater scope than in the past to promote sales of their own equipment, but the extent to which they can initiate deals or retain export earnings remains unclear.

An active arms export policy has its opponents. Prominent has been Academician V. Avduevskii, who with irony has termed it the 'export variant' of conversion. He has described the export of weapons as a 'dirty business', which often 'adds kerosene to local conflicts'. In his view, the maintenance of an export policy will simply 'drag out the agony of the militarized economy'. Furthermore, there is no guarantee that the proceeds of arms exports will not simply disappear into the 'black hole' of military production, further boosting the weapons industry.[37] There is no doubt that many associated with Soviet foreign policy have grave doubts about the compatibility of an active arms export policy and the new principles of Soviet international policy. Such reservations have been expressed, for example, by Andrei Kozyrev, now the foreign minister of the Russian republic.[38]

With problems of conversion and moves towards the market, pressure may grow for the right of enterprises to trade in arms on an independent basis. For the time being this has probably been forestalled by the so-called 'ANT' affair – a scandal involving the giant 'Uralvagonzavod' tank plant and unofficial efforts by the state-cooperative concern 'ANT' ('Avtomatizatsiya-Nauka-Tekhnika') to export a dozen 'T–72' tanks.[39] This scandal remains something of a mystery: many democratic reformers believe that the tank affair was deliberately engineered to discredit an initiative designed to promote economic reform. The basic purpose of 'ANT' was to export surplus materials and supplies, mostly held by enterprises of the defence complex, in order to import consumer goods on a large scale to ease transition to the market.[40]

As economic conditions deteriorate and some localities associated with arms production experience severe problems of supply of food and consumer goods, there are hints that thoughts are turning to the possibilities of relief through arms exports on an independent basis. There were rumours, officially denied, that the Sverdlovsk region had been granted permission to raise hard currency to import consumer goods through exports of tanks and other military hardware.[41] The government of Georgia, which regards itself as independent, made efforts to obtain guns from the Tula arms factory in exchange for food. The enterprise's director, quite correctly, referred the matter to the central authorities in Moscow. Tula is a region now experiencing extremely severe problems of supply.[42] If republics and regions gain a greater degree of autonomy in economic matters, and central ministerial control continues to weaken, it cannot be ruled out that some enterprises of the military sector may seek to ease their short-term difficulties by exporting militarily related goods.

For the market, or against?

An issue that has received increasing attention in the Soviet Union during recent months has been the overall stance of the defence industry on the question of a radical transformation of the economic system. Is it the case, as alleged by many radical democrats, that the defence complex is firmly opposed to transition to a mixed, market economy? Has it been using its power and influence to frustrate the efforts of those attempting to promote such reform? It was the appearance and then rejection of the Shatalin '500 days' programme in the early autumn of 1990 that brought these questions to the fore.

The former Ryzhkov government adopted a cautious and not always consistent approach to economic reform. The initial plan of autumn 1989, presented by Leonid Abalkin, then minister responsible for economic reform, was followed by more cautious practical measures at the end of the year. In early 1990 Gorbachev appears to have become persuaded of the need for more radical steps, with the result that the government came back with a somewhat more purposeful programme, immediately sabotaged by Ryzhkov's insistence on price increases. Up to this point, the programmes for reform contained little explicit mention of the defence sector, other than somewhat ritual reference to the importance of conversion. This changed in the summer with the Gorbachev–Yeltsin decision to convene a joint USSR–RSFSR working-group of economists, chaired by Stanislav Shatalin, to produce a more radical reform scenario.

As noted in the previous chapter, the Shatalin programme incorporated the alternative concept of conversion developed by the Yaremenko group. This envisaged the removal of most enterprises from the defence complex and the introduction of more radical measures for demilitarization. No more than 20–30 per cent of defence enterprises were to remain under the direct control of the state under a single Ministry of the Defence Industry. This is unlikely to have found favour with many of the leading administrative personnel of the defence sector, and may also have alarmed the more conservatively inclined enterprise directors. Furthermore, the programme called for a 10 per cent reduction in the military budget for 1991.[43] Central to the Shatalin programme was a radical restructuring of the union, leaving only a minimum of activities to the centre, these activities to be decided by the voluntary agreement of the republics. Such radicalism may also have alarmed the defence complex,

67

with its traditional, strongly expressed, union character.

There was a striking lack of comment on the Shatalin programme by representatives of the military sector, although there was certainly implied criticism in a collective letter to *Pravda* at the beginning of September, signed by many enterprise directors of the complex (discussed in Chapter 6).[44] However, it is not difficult to imagine that there was opposition or that leaders of the complex in positions of influence in government worked for the programme's rejection. In the event, Gorbachev refused to accept the Shatalin reform strategy, and in October the Supreme Soviet adopted the compromise 'Basic Directions' for economic stabilization and transition to the market. It has become something of a cliché in Soviet radical circles to argue that this course of events was largely determined by pressure exerted by the military-industrial complex (MIC). In the words of two members of the Academy's USA Institute: 'The onslaught [against the Shatalin programme] was powerful indeed. Some optimists believed that the days of the omnipotence of the MIC were numbered. But then all the MIC's men came out to defend it – from the prime minister to a manager of a factory in the Tambov region producing cloth for military greatcoats. Threats, insulting the "non-professionals", and downright blackmail were employed... What was the result? Overnight the President gave up the "500 days" programme.'[45] We return to this issue in the next chapter.

Although there is probably some truth in this claim, an important question remains. Was the opposition of the defence complex provoked by the specific proposals for a sharp reduction in the scale of the military sector, or was it an expression of more general antipathy towards the idea of a market, mixed economy. As suggested above, the evidence indicates that by no means all personnel of the defence industry are hostile in principle to market reforms; indeed, an increasing number are coming to see advantages from a loosening of the traditional union ministerial ties.

To a large extent it is the force of circumstances that is driving the defence industry to the market. Faced with military cuts, conversion, loss of priority and prestige, and the need to survive in conditions of growing economic dislocation, enterprise managers are resorting to new market or quasi-market institutions and practices in order to stay in business and keep their personnel in employment. In response to the inability of the centre to help, and to its perceived incompetence and indifference, new links are being forged at a local level.[46] A logic of horizontal economic relationships is beginning to displace the traditional logic of vertical administrative relations. That the Soviet defence industry is now caught up in this process is a matter of immense potential significance for the overall process of transition to a market economy: indeed, it could decide its eventual outcome.

6
THE DEFENCE INDUSTRY AS A POLITICAL FORCE

Before democratization, conversion and economic reform, the Soviet defence industry was not a conspicuous actor in the country's political life. During the Brezhnev years it was a convention that a handful of leading representatives of the sector were regularly elevated to the Central Committee of the Communist Party and the USSR Supreme Soviet. Representation normally consisted of the top party officials directly concerned with the industry, the group of industrial ministers, the chairman of the VPK, a number of leading designers and scientists of the defence sector, and the directors of a few large enterprises. Between the mid-1960s and the end of the Brezhnev period, this defence-industry group averaged approximately 4 per cent of the total membership of the Central Committee and just over 2 per cent of the delegates of the USSR Supreme Soviet.[1] There was equivalent representation at lower levels on republican, regional and city party committees and soviets. Public statements by the industry's representatives were devoted almost exclusively to non-controversial issues and rarely contained anything beyond the most muted criticism of official policy. At the same time, to an extraordinary degree, the defence sector was shielded from public criticism. For the defence industry, 'politics' was confined to the discreet committee rooms and corridors of the Central Committee building on Staraya Ploshchad', or the centre of government in the Kremlin.

Today the situation is strikingly transformed. To an ever increasing extent, the defence sector of the economy has itself become a contentious political issue. Official policies impinge negatively on the defence industry; public criticism of the MIC is unrestrained. In self-defence, the industry's representatives have been thrust into the new political arena. But, in the new circumstances of political pluralism, differences within the sector have also become more apparent: it does not speak with a single voice. Indeed, it was this fact that played a crucial role in determining the outcome of the attempted coup in August 1991.

A useful starting-point is the changing relationship between the communist party and the defence industry. One of the traditional mechanisms for ensuring the priority of the military sector was the existence within the party's organizational hierarchy of special arrangements for its oversight. As the party redefined its own role and withdrew from involvement in day-to-day economic affairs, so also, more hesitantly, did it retreat from direct intervention in the interests of the defence industry. This can be illustrated by the fate of the Central Committee Secretariat's Defence Industry Department.

The defence industry and the communist party

During most of the Brezhnev period, one of the Central Committee secretaries had responsibility for oversight of the defence industry. This was a post of some influence: Brezhnev himself occupied it for a time before becoming general secretary. Subordinate to this secretary was the Defence Industry Department, during the Brezhnev years headed first by I. D. Serbin, who occupied the post for more than twenty years, and then by I. F. Dmitriev, a long-standing associate of Dmitrii Ustinov, the defence minister. At the time when Gorbachev became general secretary, G. V. Romanov, the former Leningrad Party leader, was secretary responsible for defence industry oversight, but he soon fell to be replaced by Lev Zaikov, also from Leningrad. Yet another Leningrader, Belyakov, then replaced the seventy-five-year-old Dmitriev as head of the department. After Zaikov's appointment as Moscow city party leader in 1987, his defence-industry duties were increasingly taken over by Oleg Baklanov, formerly minister for the missile-space industry; Belyakov remained in post.

There is no doubt that the Central Committee department for the defence industry played an extremely important role in securing priority access to resources and in resolving problems of weapons production and development. In this role it worked closely with the VPK and the defence departments of Gosplan. An important concern of the department was personnel policy: the management of the *nomenklatura* system, according to which the party ensured that only its approved nominees gained appointment to posts of responsibility. But it was not only at the union level that the department operated. Similar defence-industry departments were attached to republican party central committees, and also to the party committees of regions and cities with concentrations of military-related enterprises. At all levels these departments liaised with the party committees within ministries, enterprises and R&D organizations. This hierarchy of party departments and committees formed an integral component of the administrative-command system, essential to its viable operation. Organized on a territorial basis, it provided a carefully regulated element of horizontal coordination in a system dominated by vertical, ministerial, administrative hierarchies.

In 1988 most of the departments of the Central Committee concerned with branches of the economy were disbanded. Departments were retained only for agriculture and for the defence industry, the latter being renamed the Defence Department, apparently with a somewhat wider brief embracing issues of military and disarmament policy. Similar restructuring took place at lower levels of the party: Defence Departments were retained only in major centres of military production. These arrangements probably served to retain the party's ability to ensure priority treatment for weapons production. Belyakov remained head of the Defence Department and in this capacity was made a deputy of the Congress of People's Deputies and, together with Baklanov, became a member of the Supreme Soviet's Committee for Questions of Defence and State Security. However, pressure was mounting for a clearer separation of the party from executive issues of government and the economy, as opposed to general questions of policy.

The 28th Party Congress in June 1990 marked a further decisive stage. In acknowledgment of the party's new role as one political party among many, the process of withdrawal from involvement in day-to-day practical issues was taken to its logical conclusion. Following the Congress, all the party's Central Committee departments were reorganized and converted into bodies concerned solely with policy matters. The Defence Department was disbanded.[2] For a while Baklanov retained his post as secretary concerned with military and defence-industry policy, including issues of conversion, but in April 1991 he switched from the party apparatus to the new presidential administrative structure, becoming deputy chairman of the Defence Council.[3] It appears that Belyakov and some other members of the old Defence Department also switched with Baklanov to Gorbachev's staff.

The 28th Party Congress also saw a major change in the pattern of defence-industry representation on the Central Committee, reflecting to a striking degree the party's waning influence. Gone were the ministers, the VPK chairman and almost all the leading designers and scientists; left were a few enterprise directors (at least six), now joined by a number of secretaries of party committees of defence-industry factories and institutes (again six), and a sizeable group of shopfloor workers from the sector (at least fifteen).[4] Overall, representatives of the defence industry constitute more than 7 per cent of the Committee's total membership. Some of this defence-industry group were made members of a new Central Committee Commission on the Military Policy of the CPSU, which was initially chaired by Baklanov. This Commission had a sub-commission on military-technical policy and conversion, chaired by L. L. Nikoforov, general director of the Kiev PO im. S. P. Koroleva, a major facility of the Ministry of Communications. On the whole the membership of this subcommission was undistinguished; it is difficult to imagine that it played a policy role of any real significance.[5]

As the Communist Party of the Soviet Union lost influence, some conservatively minded figures within the defence sector placed their faith in the new Russian Communist Party. It is probably no exaggeration to say that this new political formation owed its origin, at least in part, to the growing tensions within the defence industry that arose from conversion, economic reform and loss of status. The first 'initiative congress' for the formation of a Russian Party was held in Leningrad in April 1990. It was convened on the initiative of the party organizations of two production associations of the Leningrad defence industry, the 'Zavod "Arsenal"' and 'Severnaya Verf'.[6] Prominent in its convening was V. A. Tyul'kin, secretary of the party committee of the Leningrad NPO 'Avangard', a major facility of the radio industry. Tyul'kin was secretary of the organizing committee of the Congress and later became a member of the new party's Central Committee.[7] Another leading figure was Yu. Terent'ev, secretary of the 'Arsenal' party committee. The founding Congress of the new party was attended by many representatives of the defence sector. One of the first acts of the Russian Party's first leader, Ivan Polozkov, was to visit Leningrad, where he accompanied the local party first secretary, Boris Gidaspov, on a visit to the 'Bol'shevik' works of the missile industry.[8]

Given the dominant position of the Leningrad defence industry, it is not surprising that its concerns have influenced local and national politics. Successive party leaders of the city have had very close links with the military sector: Romanov at first worked in the shipbuilding industry, his successor, Zaikov, was previously general director of the NPO 'Leninets', a major concern of the radio industry. The controversial new Leningrad Party leader elected in July 1989, Gidaspov, followed in the same tradition: he was a prominent technical specialist of the munitions and rocket-fuel industry. At meetings of the Leningrad Party organization under Gidaspov, the difficulties and discontents of conversion occupied a prominent place. A factor may have been the high level of organization of the defence-industry 'lobby' within the Leningrad Party. In July 1989, a council of secretaries of primary party organization of state enterprises was formed: its leaders were drawn from prominent defence-sector associations.

It would be a mistake to conclude that all the leading party activists of the Leningrad defence industry were firmly wedded to conservative positions. The situation was more dynamic, as can be illustrated by the rapid shift of position of two prominent secretaries of party organizations of the military sector: S. Zakharov (PO 'Zavod imeni Kalinina' of the Ministry of the Defence Industry) and S. Stepanov (PO im. Kozitskogo of the Ministry of Communications). In April 1990 they were both co-signatories with V. A. Tyul'kin of an article denouncing the Democratic Platform within the party.[9] Four months later, after the 28th Party Congress, Zakharov and Stepanov joined a group of party secretaries, including others from the defence sector, in a public appeal for the foundation within the Leningrad Party of a left-centre platform in defence of reform.[10] It is possible that some of the defence-sector activists initially attracted to more conservative positions had second thoughts on further acquaintance with Polozkov's profoundly traditional and backward-looking Russian Communist Party.

As the communist party's power and influence diminished, so did its primary organizations lapse into inactivity and lost members. By the summer of 1991, there was mounting evidence that party activity and membership were in steep decline at many enterprises of the defence industry. At the vast 'Uralmash' plant in Sverdlovsk, which has some involvement in military production, by an overwhelming vote the workers called for the dissolution of the enterprise's communist party branches.[11] At the Leningrad 'Kirov' factory party membership fell by half, and the party no longer played any active role in the affairs of the plant.[12] Thus, although some party secretaries of defence-sector enterprises may have been energetically promoting conservative views, they were increasingly speaking for themselves, or at best for a diminishing band of party diehards. Not only was the communist party in decline at the enterprise level, but other new political movements and parties were beginning to take its place. For example, at the 'Kinap' factory in Samara (Kuibyshev), which is an enterprise engaged in military production, a primary organization of the Democratic Russia movement was created.[13] The same movement also organized at the Sverdlovsk 'Uralmash' works and NPO 'Avtomatika' (the workforce of the latter nominated Yeltsin for the post of president of the Russian republic), while at the Urals electro-mechanical works of the nuclear industry a branch of the Democratic Party of Russia was formed.[14] It was in this context of declining communist party influence that Boris Yeltsin decreed a ban on party workplace organization on the territory of the Russian republic. These developments all point in a single direction: even before the attempted coup, the historically close links between the Soviet defence industry and the communist party were weakening rapidly.

A defence-industry lobby?

In the autumn of 1990, it began to look as if a concerted defence-industry lobby of conservative orientation was beginning to consolidate. In early September 1990, a letter was published, addressed to the country's parliamentary bodies over the signatures of 46 general directors and general designers of organizations under the eight ministries of the

The defence industry as a political force

defence complex.[15] Significantly, this letter was published only in the party newspaper, *Pravda*. It would be interesting to know its origins: was it the product of a party initiative drawing on party contacts, possibly initiated by Baklanov and the Defence Department of the Central Committee, or was it an independent initiative from within the managerial elite of the defence sector itself?

The *Pravda* letter amounted to a plea for the maintenance of conditions permitting the defence industry to function on an effective basis. It noted that its ability to work on a stable basis was being increasingly threatened, not only by general economic disruption, but also by some recent government legislation. The letter left no doubt that the defence sector was no longer enjoying its traditional, stable, priority access to supplies of materials and equipment. The directors also complained of the destructive criticism to which the defence sector was being subjected. In the view of the signatories, it was essential to retain centralized management of the defence industry, to preserve established supply relations and the system of centralized resource allocation, and to continue state-budget funding of defence-related R&D. Finally, they appealed for legal measures preserving the status of defence-sector enterprises, including new laws 'On defence', 'On the state defence enterprise' and 'On the conversion of military production'. This unprecedented intervention left no doubt as to the growing discontent within the defence industry, and did not conceal disagreement with decisions being adopted by elected government bodies at a national and local level. As noted in Chapter 5, it may have been intended as a warning to Gorbachev and the government that the Shatalin programme for economic reform was unacceptable to important sections of the defence industry.

The emergence of a distinct defence-industry lobby of directors of establishments and other leading personnel can be traced back to 1989. It was prompted initially by cuts in military orders and dissatisfaction with policy for conversion. Local associations of state enterprises were created first in Leningrad and Moscow; from both their leading personnel and their initial concerns, there is no doubt that it was directors of enterprises of the military sector who took the lead. In Leningrad a prominent role was played by Georgii Khizha, the dynamic general director of one of the leading firms of the electronics industry, the 'Svetlana' association. The Leningrad association of state enterprises immediately made its mark by issuing a sharply worded attack on the so-called Abalkin Law – a measure of 1989 that was designed to curb the growth of wage increases.[16] The first president of the Moscow Union of State Scientific and Production Enterprises founded in October 1989 was Nikolai Mikhailov, the general director of the NPO 'Vympel', the radio industry's leading development organization for over-the-horizon radar systems. One of the first acts of the union was the drafting of a Law on Conversion, the text of which was submitted to the USSR Supreme Soviet.[17]

In the following months, similar associations were set up in other cities and regions, culminating in the formation of an Association of State Enterprises and Associations of the USSR. This body embraced both civil and defence-sector enterprises, but the lead was taken by the latter. The president was Aleksandr Tizyakov, since 1977 general director of the aviation industry's Sverdlovsk PO 'Zavod imeni Kalinina', an important centre for the development of missiles, including cruise-missile systems. In November 1990, Tizyakov was described by the Russian prime minister, Ivan Silaev (a former aviation-industry minister), as a highly qualified and experienced organizer, but one who 'sticks to conservative positions'.[18] A communist of unshaken conviction, Tizyakov energetically defended the interests of the enterprises of the state sector of industry. He denied that it was his intervention on behalf of the defence industry in early October 1990 that was responsible for persuading Gorbachev to drop his support for the Shatalin '500 days' programme, although a meeting with the president did take place, and Tizyakov did not conceal his hostility to the programme, describing it as 'illiterate and absolutely absurd'.[19]

The all-union association hit the headlines in December 1990 when it held a national conference with Gorbachev, Ryzhkov and other leaders in attendance at the 3,000-strong gathering. The meeting was striking for the openly expressed concern at the state of the economy and the strong support for extreme measures for stabilization. Some speakers displayed an ill-concealed nostalgia for the traditional administrative-command methods of running the economy. Overall, the gathering adopted a toughly worded appeal to the president and the country's parliamentary bodies, calling for urgent, extraordinary measures to stabilize the economy and to preserve the single, union economy.[20] Gorbachev received a hostile reception and must have been left in no doubt that the patience of many leaders of industry was becoming exhausted.

The conservatism of this elite group of the Soviet economy was underlined by the findings of an opinion poll of the conference participants. No less than 91 per cent of directors polled wanted the introduction of extraordinary measures to stabilize the economy. The private ownership of enterprises was supported by only 16 per cent; and cooperatives by 24 per cent. However, an interesting generational difference emerged. Whereas three-quarters of the older generation of directors saw the state enterprise as the main vehicle for the future development of the economy, the younger generation overwhelmingly backed joint stock and small enterprises.[21] Although the majority of those polled were in favour of the adoption of market reforms, 35 per cent supported the retention of planning in leading branches of the economy (including, presumably, the defence industry). But only 10 per cent favoured centralized economic management of the traditional type.[22]

Shortly before the meeting of the national association, the directors of state enterprises achieved a notable step in their efforts to influence government policy. A Council of Ministers decree of 27 November 1990 provided for the establishment of a Council of Leaders of State Enterprises, Associations and Organizations as a consultative body reporting directly to Prime Minister Ryzhkov. One of its tasks was specified as monitoring and preparing recommendations on defence-industry conversion. The membership of the council testified to the considerable influence of the defence industry: at least 40 per cent of the 37 members were directors of associations and enterprises of the defence complex, including such well-known figures as Tizyakov and Mikhailov.[23] Of the defence-sector directors, 80 per cent headed enterprises located in Russia. It is interesting that none of the defence-sector council members was a member of either the CPSU or Russian Communist Party Central Committees, and only one (Mikhailov) was a signatory of the September 6th protest letter to *Pravda*.

This new grouping soon made its views known in dramatic fashion. Almost all the defence-industry members of the Council of Leaders of State Enterprises, including Tizyakov and Mikhailov, put their signatures to a remarkable letter to Gorbachev at the time of the Fourth Congress of People's Deputies of the USSR at the end of 1990. The letter presented an apocalyptic view of the state of the nation and urged Gorbachev to use his presidential powers to the full to restore stability and discipline, if necessary by resort to states of emergency in regions of conflict. This 'letter of the 53' – the other signatories of which included Moiseev, chief of the general staff, V. I. Varennikov, commander-in-chief of the ground forces, Baklanov, Gidaspov, a group of defence-sector scientists and designers, and some writers of Russian nationalist leaning including Aleksandr Prokhanov, the favourite of the military conservatives – played a role in creating the climate of conservatism that culminated in the resignation of Eduard Shevardnadze as foreign minister and the military action in the Baltic republics early in the new year.[24] Also, early in 1991, the members of the Council of Leaders of State Enterprises had a meeting with Gorbachev: not surprisingly questions of discipline and order figured prominently.[25]

These events of late 1990 gave the impression that the managerial elite of the defence industry was consolidating into a conservative political force that was opposed to further democratization and radical economic transformation. However, as subsequent developments have shown, this impression was only partially correct. An important new factor was the rapid rise to prominence of a much broader organization representing the interests of the country's managerial and technical elite, namely the Scientific and Industrial Union of the USSR under the leadership of its president, Arkadii Vol'skii. Created in June 1990, this union includes as one of its constituent organizations the national Association of State Enterprises, but it also embraces bodies representing the interests of the growing non-state sector: unions of cooperatives, entrepreneurs and joint ventures. The union is committed to promoting the interests of industry and science in the conditions of a market economy, and to helping form the institutional infrastructure of such an economy. Its ten vice-presidents include leading figures of the defence sector: Mikhailov, Igor' Seleznev (general designer of the aviation industry's 'Raduga' design bureau at Dubna), Evgenii Velikhov, Academy of Sciences vice-president and director of the nuclear industry's Kurchatov Institute, and, until the attempted coup, Tizyakov.[26] Overall the Scientific and Industrial Union has been much more positive in its support for market reform and privatization than the Association of State Enterprises. In recognition of the specific features of the defence complex, however, Vol'skii has spoken in favour of a cautious approach to its marketization.[27]

By the summer of 1991 the divergence of positions within the defence sector had become manifest. Whereas Tizyakov was maintaining his conservative stance, openly expressing hostility to privatization and cooperatives and insisting that any market had to be 'socialist', other leading figures were backing democratic change.[28] Vol'skii was one of the founder members of the Movement for Democratic Reform launched in July 1991 by Shevardnadze, Yakovlev, Silaev and other prominent reformers. A number of people's deputies and leaders of regional associations of state enterprises, including prominent figures of the defence industry, immediately made known their support for the new movement. Those involved include Seleznev, Velikhov, Mikhailov, his successor as president of the Moscow association Igor Artyukh (general director of NPO 'Torii'), and Khizha of Leningrad.[29] Reflecting the fluidity of the situation in the country, Artyukh and Mikhailov appear to have quickly modified their political positions: only six months earlier they had been signatories of the notorious 'letter of the 53'. Thus, in the run-up to the dramatic events of August 1991, although sharing certain common professional concerns, representatives of the managerial and technical elite of the military sector found themselves on different sides of the political divide.

For the Soviet Union or Russia?

The defence industry has also emerged as a factor in the complex politics of nationalism, not only in the Baltic and other republics with strong movements for independence, but also within Russia itself. Here we must consider the difficult issue of the extent to which the defence industry is perceived to be a bastion of Russian or, more generally, Slavic interests within the multinational state of the USSR. Or is it rather the case that the defence sector is seen to be a significant force representing the 'union' interest in favour of the retention of a single Soviet state? Perhaps this is a false dichotomy: in the terms of some of today's Soviet radicals, the MIC may constitute a central pillar of the Soviet Russian 'imperial' order.

Almost all the enterprises and research organizations of the defence industry are subordinated to all-union ministries. These highly centralized ministries of the defence complex represent the very core of the traditional Soviet system of industrial administration. Also characteristic of the defence sector are the elaborate nationwide networks of supply that are essential to the industry's successful operation. In these circumstances it is not surprising that leading personnel of the defence complex have tended to adopt strongly pro-union positions, opposed to developments threatening the integrity of the economic system of the country.

The involvement of defence-industry representatives in the formation of the Russian Communist Party has already been mentioned. But there have also been examples of attempts to identify the defence complex directly with conservative Russian nationalism. From within the industry, a prominent exponent of this view has been the missile designer Sergei Nepobedimyi, who for many years headed a major facility at Kolomna, southeast of Moscow. For Nepobedimyi, a critic of conversion, the USSR's defence industry is Slavic in character.[30] A similar position has been implicit in the writings of the novelist Alekasandr Prokhanov. He has written scathingly of the destruction of the Russian defence industry through ill-considered conversion, realized, in his view, by 'anti-national, anti-state means'.[31] That the country's defence industry is being wrecked through irresponsibly implemented conversion is also the view of the well-known fundamentalist communist Nina Andreeva, who also believes that it is the historic mission of the Slavs to prevent the destruction of the 'heroic efforts of the Bolsheviks'.[32] The writings of Prokhanov have provided plenty of grist to the mill of those radical democrats who have maintained that the MIC is a profoundly conservative and anti-democratic formation. The role of the defence industry in the Baltic republics provided further evidence for this view.

Events in the Baltic republic have illustrated well the stance of sections of the defence industry. Although there does not appear to be much, if any, end-product weapons production in Estonia, Latvia and Lithuania, there are important research and production facilities for military-related equipment and components. In all three republics there are major producers of electronic, radio and communications equipment, while Estonia has enterprises of the nuclear industry. These defence-complex facilities form the core of the set of union enterprises that play a substantial role in the economic life of the three Baltic states.

In all three republics, leading representatives of the defence sector have been prominent in the creation of organizations promoting pro-union positions, which are opposed to the local movements for independence. In Estonia, for example, a prominent figure has been Vladimir Yarovoi, general director of the nuclear industry's Tallinn PO 'Gosudarstvennyi soyuznyi zavod "Dvigatel"', a major plant of the republic employing several thousand workers, many of Russian origin. From the beginning of the active nationalist movement in the republic, Yarovoi emerged as a forceful advocate of the pro-union position and was elected chairman of the United Council of Labour Collectives of Estonia, a body committed to the defence of interests of the Russian population of the republic. Later Yarovoi, one of the *sredmashevtsy* (personnel of the Minsredmash), became leader of a newly created Committee for the Defence of Union Power and Civil Rights.[33] Many of the defence plants of the Baltic republics have a high proportion of Russian workers, and it is not surprising that they should have become centres for various 'interfront' organizations.

The Moscow ministries have made strenuous efforts to keep these union plants under their control, resisting vigorously any moves to transfer them to republican subordination. However, some of the enterprises concerned have adopted less clear-cut positions. Two distinct, but closely related, issues have come to the forefront: union subordination and the question of ownership. Moscow has wanted to retain control, but some enterprise managements have seen advantage in the greater independence afforded by joint stock companies and other new forms of ownership. In Lithuania, for example, V. Kasatkin, the general director of a defence-sector plant, the PO 'Pyargale', is president of the republic's Association of Free Enterprises, seeking to promote non-state forms of ownership.[34] Similarly 'Integral', the USSR Supreme Soviet's attempt to establish an association of union enterprises of Estonia, was not met with enthusiasm by all the directors of the plants concerned. Managers and workers have come to appreciate the advantages offered by republican subordination. The activities of union enterprises of the defence industry have been regulated by inflexible rules established in Moscow. In particular this applies to rates of pay: in the autumn of 1990, a lathe operator at the 'Dvigatel'' works in Estonia was earning no more than 300 roubles per month; at an enterprise under republican control 600 roubles could be earned![35]

At the 28th Congress of the CPSU in the summer of 1990, representa-

The defence industry as a political force

tives of three of the major defence-industry enterprises of the Baltic republics (Vilnius PO im. 60–letiya Oktyabrya, Riga PO 'VEF' and Tallinn PO 'Punane RET') were elected to the CPSU Central Committee. The general director of the Vilnius plant, O. Burdenko, was to play an active role in the events of January 1991: the head enterprise of his association was identified as the headquarters of the republic's self-styled 'national salvation front'. Defence plants also played a prominent role in the strike movements of early 1991, although there were reports that some workers had been under pressure from management to participate in strikes and demonstrations.

The Baltic events also provided additional evidence that enterprises of the defence complex cannot be classed simply as bastions of conservatism. In Leningrad, workers at several major military-sector plants took part in symbolic strike action to protest at the deaths in Lithuania; these workers included employees of the 'Kirovskii zavod', 'Azimut', 'Vektor' and 'Pozitron' associations.[36]

It is not only in the Baltic republics that leaders of the defence industry have championed the interests of the Russian section of the population and promoted pro-union policies. According to a leader of the Kazakh civic movement 'Azat', most of the members of the 'Edinstvo' ('Unity') movement of Kazakhstan are employees of the defence industry, with more than forty defence-complex enterprises being affiliated on a collective basis. It is claimed that the workers of these all-union plants, which employ very few Kazakhs, have for many years enjoyed a privileged position in terms of pay and welfare provision, and that the enterprises have taken little notice of the local authorities. As the republic strives for sovereignty, representatives of the defence industry 'are afraid of losing their old comforts. They like living and working in Kazakhstan, but taking orders from Moscow. It suits them.'[37]

The defence industry has also figured prominently in the politics of the Russian republic. From his time in Sverdlovsk, Boris Yeltsin must have acquired considerable knowledge of the military sector, and it is notable that he has not indulged in the generalized criticism of the defence industry that has been so common in radical circles. Indeed, in his autobiography he went out of his way to note the support that he had received from workers of the defence complex.[38] In Moscow, some of his most active support has come from the citizens of the electronics science

83

town of Zelenograd, and, as noted above, he was nominated for the post of Russian president by the workforce of a leading Sverdlovsk defence-industry facility. On a visit to the Leningrad Kirov factory in March 1991, Yeltsin declared that it was a 'myth' that the entire MIC was hindering transition to the market, in fact 'the MIC is heterogeneous'.[39] During his presidential electoral campaign, Yeltsin visited several centres of military production, including Tula and Voronezh, and took care to address the problems being experienced by workers at plants that were undergoing conversion. Although many radicals attempted to present Ryzhkov as the candidate of the MIC, the patterns of voting suggest that this was not the perception of its rank-and-file. Yeltsin received the overwhelming support of the electorate in such important centres of military production as Leningrad, Moscow and Sverdlovsk. Indeed, in Leningrad Yeltsin received more than two-thirds of the vote, compared with a mere 10 per cent for Ryzhkov.[40]

As a former minister of the aviation industry and later head of the civil machinebuilding complex, the Russian prime minister, Silaev, has an insider's knowledge and a keen awareness of the superior competence of the defence industry. In seeking to enhance the economic independence of Russia, rather than to confront the powerful defence sector of the republic, Silaev has attempted to persuade the leaders of its enterprises of the advantages of cooperation with the Russian authorities. It is this concern that probably explains the attitude towards the defence sector adopted by Yeltsin and the Russian government. In the words of the journal *Kommersant*, 'now, with general economic collapse, the military-industrial complex is becoming less loyal to the centre, which can no longer finance it without limit. In such conditions the Russian leader is striving to drive a wedge between the MIC and the Kremlin.'[41] This cautious, differentiated approach of the Russian government has not been shared, however, by all those committed to radical, democratic change.

Radical perspectives
In the months preceding the attempted coup, many radical reformers came to identify the MIC as one of the principal sources of conservatism in Soviet society, alongside the armed forces, the KGB and the commun-

ist party. By late 1990 it had become a shibboleth of radicals that the Ryzhkov government was simply a government of the defence industry. Addressing a demonstration in Moscow in September 1990, Gavriil Popov, mayor of the city, called for the resignation of the Ryzhkov government: 'This Council of Ministers was formed by the Politburo, and it is the final embodiment of the monopoly of power of the CPSU. The Council of Ministers was and is the government of the military-industrial complex.'[42] It has been widely held that pressure exerted by the MIC led to rejection of the Shatalin '500 days' programme for economic reform. The economist Petrakov claimed that the new Cabinet of Ministers of Pavlov was also dominated by the MIC, making it impossible to tackle the problem of inflation.[43] In short, the defence industry has been seen as a 'monster', a vast unaccountable monolith, blocking the path to the market and democracy.[44]

This perception of the influence of the defence industry has derived to no small extent from the secrecy that has surrounded its activities, and in particular from inadequate public knowledge of its true scale and role in the economy. Radical reformers have been prone to exaggerate the size of the defence sector, at times to the point of absurdity. The critical faculties of even the most respected scholars have become blunted when confronted with the mysteries of the armaments industry. The crude estimates offered by individual scholars have tended quickly to become common currency; the authorities, for their part, have countered only by repeating the well-known, but flawed, official figures. Examples are legion. The well-known historian Yurii Afanas'ev, leader of the Interregional Group of Deputies, has claimed that the MIC probably employs over half the people of the Soviet Union and that, in the Russian republic, factories and plants of the complex employ 82 per cent of the population.[45] Another extreme example is the claim of one author, V. Pervyshin, that industrial output to the value of 455 billion roubles, half of the annual total, is delivered to the MIC 'moloch', as well as to the armed forces, KGB and Ministry of Internal Affairs. Also, Pervyshin maintains that total military expenditure, apparently in current Soviet prices, represents no less than 52 per cent of GNP![46]

The defence industry is undoubtedly a powerful force in Soviet society, a significant interest group able to exert strong political influence. But, in seeking to pin all, or at least a large share, of the blame for the leadership's irresolution in reform onto the defence industry, many radicals have manifested a mode of thought all too common in Soviet history: the identification of scapegoats – dark, sinister forces striving to hold back the march of progress. More sober voices have warned of the political dangers of such demonization. Lilya Shevtsova, for example, a perceptive observer of the Soviet political scene, has pointed out that the defence industry is not a monolithic conservative force. Within it, she observes, are diverse groups with their own particular concerns. Moreover, a tendency is emerging among such groups to see the market as 'not the worst evil', and they are therefore prepared to consider a 'new political roof'. Similar differentiation, she believes, is apparent within the armed forces. Hence, 'it would be completely incorrect to regard this or that institution of Soviet society as being an embodiment of reaction alone. In fact, the lack of a differentiated approach to the institutions of the old system on the part of the democratic forces has to no small degree facilitated the offensive of the counter-reformation.'[47] Three months after Shevtsova's warning, the forces of the counter-reformation made their desperate bid for power.

The defence industry and the August 1991 coup

In the early hours of 19 August 1991, power was seized by a small group of conspirators under the nominal leadership of Vice-President Gennadii Yanaev. The self-proclaimed State Committee for the State of Emergency (SCSE) included not only the minister of defence, Dmitrii Yazov, the chairman of the KGB, Vladimir Kryuchkov, the minister of internal affairs, Boris Pugo, and the prime minister, Valentin Pavlov, but also two figures well-known for their close association with the defence industry, namely Oleg Baklanov and Aleksandr Tizyakov.

The involvement of Baklanov and Tizyakov, especially of the latter, was not entirely unexpected. Both had been signatories of the December 1990 'letter of the 53', and, only a month prior to the coup attempt, Tizyakov was one of twelve prominent conservatives who signed an impassioned 'Appeal to the People', published in *Sovetskaya Rossiya*, the newspaper of the Russian communists. This appeal, also signed by two other active participants in the putsch – Deputy Defence Minister Valentin Varennikov and the chairman of the USSR Peasants' Union,

Vasilii Starodubtsev – called for the launching of a popular patriotic movement to prevent the destruction of the motherland.[48] There is little doubt that the principal instigator of this movement, and also of the earlier 'letter of the 53', was the writer Aleksandr Prokhanov, the 'nightingale of the general staff'. It was Prokhanov who revealed, four days before the attempted coup, that a national congress of the patriotic movement would be convened towards the end of September.[49] Perhaps the organizers of the coup were panicked into premature action by a sooner-than-expected agreement on a new Union Treaty.

The first decree of the SCSE called for measures to restore order to the economy that were strongly reminiscent of the emergency action demanded by Tizyakov's Association of State Enterprises at its meeting nine months earlier. Above all, it emphasized the importance of enterprises meeting in full their supply obligations. This demand for a partial restoration of the command system was coupled with populist declarations of intent to reduce the prices of some consumer goods and to raise the pay of some categories of workers.[50]

At the time of writing, the attitude of the leadership of the defence industry to the attempted coup remains unclear. From reports of the meeting of the Cabinet of Ministers convened by Pavlov on the first day, it appears that no ministers of the defence complex expressed a view, possibly because none were present. Maslyukov, the chairman of the VPK, was present and is reported to have raised questions and also to have had a wrangle with Pavlov.[51] Later he met the members of the SCSE and informed them that, although the defence industry was working normally, enterprises were raising more and more questions about the creation of the emergency committee.[52] By this time, Maslyukov was probably aware of the strong resistance to the attempted coup in such important centres of the defence industry as Moscow, Leningrad and Sverdlovsk. The leaders of all the large enterprises of Sverdlovsk, for example, refused to recognize the SCSE and declared support for the stand of Yelsin's Russian government. Workers at some enterprises, including 'Uralmash', went on strike in protest. At Tizyakov's own enterprise, the NPO 'Zavod imeni Kalinina', speakers at a meeting of the workforce declared their general director a state criminal and called for his arrest – a call that was soon satisfied.[53]

In the immediate aftermath of the failed seizure of power, representatives of the pro-reform wing of the defence industry quickly rose to prominence. Under the leadership of the Russian prime minister, Silaev, an interim committee was formed for the operational management of the economy. Arkadii Vol'skii, president of the Scientific and Industrial Union, took over responsibility for oversight of the work of industry, including the defence sector. Co-opted members of the committee included N. Mikhailov, general director of the radio industry's NPO 'Vympel' and a vice-president of the union, and Viktor Protasov, a prominent scientist of the defence industry and director of the Central Research Institute of Special Machinebuilding.[54] As already noted, a month earlier Mikhailov had declared his support for the new Movement for Democratic Reform, of which Vol'skii was one of the founders.

There is little doubt that the attempt to take power and to reverse the processes of reform arose in part from the discontents of the military and the defence industry. In taking their desperate action, Baklanov, Tizyakov and the other conspirators probably believed that they would have the backing of all those demoralized by military cuts, the chaotic process of conversion, economic disintegration and an inexorable break-up of the structures of the union. They miscalculated. To a considerable extent the coup failed because not only had traditional institutions been fractured and priorities altered during six years of perestroika, but attitudes had also undergone significant change. Within the very heart of the military-industrial complex the principles of democracy, citizenship, nationhood and the market had taken root. By August 1991, the divergence of attitudes within the defence industry, discussed above, paralleled by similar processes within the armed forces, the communist party, and, probably, also the KGB, was such that it deprived the conspirators of the support which, in the past, they might have been justified in taking for granted. The defeat of the attempted coup, the collapse of the communist party and the general weakening of the forces of conservatism open the way for a genuine, far-reaching transformation of the Soviet defence industry.

7
PROSPECTS AND IMPLICATIONS FOR THE WEST

The processes of conversion and reform now underway in the Soviet defence industry have large potential implications for the West. From the point of view of security, the transition to lower levels of output of military hardware is to be welcomed and, together with developments in arms control – notably the Conventional Forces in Europe treaty and the START treaty to reduce strategic nuclear forces – should contribute to the evolution of a safer, post-cold-war world. But there are also economic implications of some importance. Notwithstanding all the current difficulties of conversion, moderation of the growth of armaments production should assist the revitalization of the Soviet economy, with potential benefits to the West in terms of a more stable world economic order, while the opening-up of the defence industry is already providing new opportunities for trade and cooperation. However, in both areas there remain many uncertainties: it will inevitably take time before the new order is consolidated, and it cannot be said that the processes of change are yet irreversible.

Conversion and security
A number of considerations must enter into any assessment of the security implications of recent developments. So far, the strategy of conversion has been one designed to conserve the basic capability of the

Soviet defence industry. As noted in Chapter 4, very few facilities are undergoing complete conversion, and at the remainder the potential is being retained for a resumed expansion of military production in the event of perceived need. In some cases facilities for weapons manufacture are simply being mothballed. The military have been unwilling to reconsider the traditional policy for the mobilizational preparedness of the economy, but at least the issue is now on the agenda for debate. It may be significant that towards the end of 1990, at a time when the revised State Conversion Programme was being considered by the Presidential Council, the deputy minister of defence for armaments, Vitalii Shabanov, was replaced by his younger first deputy, Vyacheslav Mironov.[1] Shabanov was evidently unhappy with many aspects of military cuts and conversion: it is possible that his replacement signalled a shift in thinking.[2] Regardless of the significance of this change, the principle of reversibility of conversion has been widely challenged and, together with growing presssure for more decisive demilitarization, this could yet lead to more radical measures that are more reassuring from the point of view of Western security.

Another important issue is the extent to which the changes underway could eventually result in a somewhat smaller Soviet defence industry, but one capable of developing and producing weapons of a higher technological level and quality. Since the new military leaders, Evgenii Shaposhnikov and Vladimir Lobov, chief of the general staff, are committed to an early professionalization of the armed services, it is likely that they will press for qualitatively improved hardware to meet the needs of smaller, but more highly trained, forces. However, given the forces now at work for economic dislocation, the difficulties and uncertainties of economic reform, the problems of conversion and the general lack of progress in the modernization of the civilian economy since the mid–1980s, it is difficult to envisage such an outcome as a realistic possibility during the remainder of this century. It is true that the increasing commercial contacts with the West in the fields of electronics, computing and information technologies in general should help to raise the country's technological level in a manner that could assist the military sector in its modernization efforts, but time will be needed to translate these gains into deployable military systems.

A problem now facing the Soviet armed forces and the defence industry is an amplification of the budgetary squeeze by the pressure of rising costs. In the past the Soviet military has benefitted from economies associated with large-volume manufacture of basic weapon systems. This production covered not only domestic procurement needs, but also substantial exports to Warsaw Pact partners and friends in the Third World. Now shorter production runs of military hardware are beginning to result in higher costs. In discussion of the budget for 1991, there were claims that this had become a serious problem: the per unit cost of a tank, for example, was higher by 14 per cent.[3] This is one of the reasons why the military were so unhappy with the eventual outcome of the budgetary process. Their concern was heightened by the fact that inflation is also beginning to bite into an already reduced budget for R&D. Costs are rising in the R&D sector, partly because higher salaries are being paid to research personnel without appropriate budgetary compensation. Institutes are being forced to offer better rewards in an effort to retain skilled personnel, who are being tempted by the greater freedom and earnings potential now offered by the cooperatives, small enterprises and joint ventures, not to speak of emerging possibilities for employment abroad. But R&D organizations, faced with funding cuts and increasing pressure for profitable operation, are also seeking to cover their costs through higher charges for their services. Mironov, the new deputy minister for armaments, has expressed his grave concern that cost pressures are leading to a reduction in the number of performed military R&D projects.[4] These pressures are unlikely to diminish: the real magnitude of military cuts is likely to be larger than indicated by the scale of budget cuts, further impairing the ability of the Soviet defence industry to keep abreast of technical developments in the West. In these circumstances it is not surprising that some would like to call a halt to the relentless erosion of the military sector's capability.

In the post-Gulf-war situation there is a new uncertainty. Almost immediately, while the fighting was still underway, voices began to be raised questioning the wisdom of military cuts and the conversion policy in the light of the very evident achievements from the use of high-technology weapons by the anti-Iraq coalition forces. One of the first to question the conversion policy was Boris Gidaspov, Leningrad Party chief, in the communist party's weekly paper *Glasnost'*. In particular, Gidaspov expressed concern that there could be serious consequences for Soviet security of reduced levels of expenditure on military R&D.[5] Some leaders of the armed forces also expressed their concern. Dmitri T. Yazov, the defence minister, called for a complete review of the Soviet air defence system and it is not difficult to imagine that such a review could find a need for new, research-intensive, technical solutions.[6] Although there must be a danger that the Gulf war will create conditions favourable to those wishing to moderate or even reverse the military cuts and conversion policy, it is by no means evident that this will be the outcome. Even from within the military there will be other voices urging more radical measures to revitalize the economy, understanding that rapid transition to an effective market economy is the best means of creating the potential to respond to any new military, technical challenge should the need arise.

Cooperative conversion

In undertaking defence-industry conversion, the Soviet authorities from the outset made clear their desire for international cooperation. Gorbachev on visits abroad has stressed the potential benefits of collaboration and has attempted to alert Western business interests to the new commercial possibilities created by military reductions. High-level delegations from the Soviet defence industry have now visited many leading Western countries, including Britain, in search both of ideas for easing the conversion process, and of new business partners. In some cases, including Italy, France and Japan, intergovernmental agreements have been concluded for cooperation in conversion-related activities. A call for assistance in converting the military sector also figured prominently in Gorbachev's presentation to the Group of Seven leaders in London in July 1991.

In Soviet efforts to find Western partners, an important place has been occupied by exhibitions of the achievements of the defence complex. To date the largest has been the 'Conversion–90' exhibition mounted in Munich in April 1990. This was a unique display of 1,200 products and technologies developed and produced by 300 organizations of the defence-industry ministries.[7] It could be argued that the exhibition was misnamed: most of the items on display were not the outcome of conversion as such, but represented achievements of the well-established civil side of the Soviet defence industry. Nevertheless, 'Conversion–90' was important in establishing the credentials of the Soviet military sector in terms of its capability of generating high-grade technologies of potential interest to Western companies. For many technical specialists and managers of the Soviet defence industry it provided the first opportunity for direct contact with foreigners, and, although unsuccessful from a commercial point of view, the exhibition served a useful function in helping to change attitudes on both sides. A similar, but more comprehensive, 'Conversion–91' exhibition is being organized in Bologna, Italy, in September 1991 and is likely to feature more examples of genuine conversion.[8]

Other exhibitions within the Soviet Union have featured the technical achievements of the aerospace industry, including the aero-engine branch, and some of the new food-industry equipment developed by defence-industry establishments during the past three years. Abroad, apart from the showing of Soviet military and civil aircraft at air displays in many countries, exhibitions have included presentations of advanced materials associated with space and military programmes.

The new possibilities of commercial links are best exemplified by developments in the aerospace industry. In a calculated effort to reduce the impact of conversion, the aircraft industry has pursued a successful policy of establishing joint projects with Western partners in the field of civil aviation. Above all, the industry sought to prevent its facilities being switched to activities unconnected with the building of aircraft. This concern was greatest for design organizations heavily involved in military work, including the Sukhoi, Mikoyan and Tupolev bureaux, and some of the engine-development organizations with a strong military orientation.

Notable among the joint projects now underway is the Sukhoi–Gulfstream (USA) collaboration in the development of supersonic executive jets, with engines to be supplied as a result of joint work by Rolls-Royce and the Moscow NPO 'Saturn', the former Lyulka aero-engine design organization.[9] Another interesting civil aviation project is a Sukhoi venture with a company in Singapore for the development of an original surface-effect plane, the 'Ekranolet'.[10] More ambitious is the joint project of British Aerospace and the Antonov design organization in Kiev for launching the 'Hotol' space vehicle from the world's largest aircraft, the An–225.[11]

In the space-missile industry there have been efforts to expand foreign collaboration in civil space technology. The Dnepropetrovsk NPO 'Yuzhnoe', for example, a major centre for the development and production of missiles and space launchers, has formed a new commercial division 'Yuzhkosmos', one of the functions of which is to secure orders from abroad for the use of the 'Zenit' launcher.[12] Foreign companies have become involved in a number of joint ventures with organizations of the Ministry of General Machinebuilding. The fields covered include advanced materials, medical equipment, computers, equipment for the food industry and consumer goods. Notable examples include a joint venture, involving the 'Bol'shevik' missile plant in Leningrad and a US company, for the production of invalid carriages, and an Italian–Soviet joint venture for the production of composite materials for the food and chemical industries involving the missile-space industry's principal centre for advanced materials, the NPO 'Kompozit' near Moscow.[13]

Joint ventures have also been organized in the nuclear industry. One of the first was a joint venture, 'Svetozor', for the manufacture of 'Polaroid' instant cameras. This involves facilities of the former Minsredmash in Moscow, Podol'sk and Estonia.[14] Western firms are also becoming involved in projects to provide new civil employment in the former 'closed' towns. In the shipbuilding industry, hitherto ultra-secret plants are now being visited by foreigners who are concluding deals for civil projects. In February 1991, for example, the vast Severodvinsk submarine yard was visited by Dutch, Belgian and Danish businessmen. Contracts were signed for the building of ten self-propelled barges for river transport.[15] The shipbuilding ministry has also been engaged in discussion of a major deal with a Western consortium, the Geneva-based 'Inter-Maritime Management', for export-orientated commercial shipbuilding at Soviet shipyards, in some cases using capacity freed by reduced naval orders. Companies involved in this project include the British 'Swan-Hunter' and 'Appledore'. However, this deal is not without its critics: the Leningrad authorities, for example, see it as an attempt by the ministry to retain its monopoly position and fear that it will limit their freedom of action in relation to the development of local shipyards.[16]

As conversion deepens, new business opportunities are likely to appear. One field that could offer genuinely profitable opportunities is the exploitation of hitherto classified technologies developed for military and space programmes. As noted in Chapter 4, there is now an active transfer policy coupled with a process of opening-up previously secret facilities. A problem for many Western firms is inadequate information on the technologies on offer. The information provided by Soviet organizations can often be insufficiently detailed to provide an adequate basis for commercial decisions. It is indicative, however, that in September 1990 when South Korean industry was provided with details about a hundred previously classified defence-sector technologies, 43 were evaluated as usable and a further 35 usable after further research.[17]

Most institutes and enterprises of the defence industry are still subject to strict ministerial control and have to contend with a variety of inhibitions constraining commercial contacts with foreign firms. Although reduced in severity and scope, secrecy remains a major consideration, with the KGB ever vigilant for breaches by over-enthusiastic enterprise personnel. There have been cases of defence-sector organizations making their own direct approaches to foreign companies and then encountering strong official disapproval. Some Western companies have had difficulty in visiting facilities with which they are attempting to enter into business relations. There are also restrictions on the right of military-related organizations to sell licences for technology to foreign clients. For more effective foreign involvement in conversion, the Soviet authorities will have to ease such restrictions and switch to a system according to which secrecy applies only to matters of genuine concern to national security.

What is emerging in the Soviet Union is an official position which closely links the issues of security and international cooperation in conversion. Extensive foreign involvement in conversion and the development of large-scale international projects involving the Soviet defence industry are seen as means of enhancing confidence in the irreversibility of both the disarmament process and the transition to a new order within the USSR. This linkage is implicit in many of Gorbachev's pronouncements and has been argued explicitly by Deputy Foreign Minister Viktor Karpov and others.[18] The hope is clearly that such international cooperation will facilitate further demilitarization of the Soviet economy and possibly also that it will make it more difficult for any conservative forces to put the processes of reform into reverse.

An uncertain future

The prospects for the defence sector of the Soviet economy depend to a considerable extent on the broader conditions of economic and political development, and for this reason must remain uncertain. But, as this study has sought to demonstrate, the defence complex is itself a principal actor in the unfolding drama of Soviet development in post-communist times. It has the power and influence to undermine progress towards a market, mixed economy, and is well-placed to have an important say in the new structure of the union: in the short term the single most pressing political issue. Decisions adopted during recent years have also put the defence industry into a position where it can determine the success or failure of efforts to improve the living standards of Soviet citizens. As already noted, these developments have served to increase the size of the defence complex and to enhance its policy influence. This is the paradoxical outcome of Gorbachev's efforts to reduce the military burden that is crippling the Soviet economy.

The present situation cannot be considered stable. It is difficult to avoid the conclusion that further measures for demilitarization of the economy are essential if progress in reform is to be maintained. A major obstacle is the lack of reliable information on the true resource cost of the country's military effort. It is doubtful whether Gorbachev or any other government leader has anything other than an impressionistic view of the true scale of the defence sector and its real share of industrial output. This element of mystery has served the military and defence industry well during several decades, and it must be acknowledged that it will be no easy matter to establish the truth. But a more accurate assessment of the burden would facilitate the political task of securing backing for more decisive measures, in particular removal from the defence complex of all but the most vital core facilities essential to the maintenance of the country's legitimate security needs. As Karpov has stressed, the provision of accurate and full information on the Soviet defence industry would also facilitate greatly efforts to secure international cooperation in the realization of conversion.[19]

Meanwhile, in the absence of accurate data, exaggerated claims gain wide currency, fuelling popular antagonism to the MIC. Some of this opposition is nihilistic in character, apparently denying any legitimate role for weapons development and production. Such maximalism serves only to strengthen conservative and imperial sentiments at the other political pole. What is required is more sober, better-informed discussion: here Soviet academic specialists have a major responsibility.

A possibility that must now be faced in any discussion of prospects for the USSR is the break-up of the union. What would happen to the Soviet defence industry if the federation could not be preserved? Independence for the Baltic republics, Georgia and Moldavia would create transitional problems, especially if all established economic links were broken, but would not seriously impair the functioning of the Soviet defence complex. It would be a very different matter if the breakup extended to the Ukraine or Kazakhstan. Both republics play vital roles and have countless links with enterprises and R&D organizations of the Russian federation. Indeed, the impact of break-up would be so severe that it is difficult to imagine that it would be permitted by the remaining union, or Russian, political and military authorities. On the other hand, any republic, apart from Russia and possibly the Ukraine, that embarked on an independent path of development would have great difficulty in establishing its own viable defence industry from the disparate, unrelated fragments it would inherit. One is forced to conclude that the structure of the Soviet defence industry represents a factor likely to prompt efforts to retain some form of common economic and security community, however loosely framed.

The Soviet Union is a country that for most of its history has possessed a unique sense of its own destiny. This was the world's first socialist country, the flagship of a new social order the superior merits of which would eventually be demonstrated to the peoples of the world. Developing in defiance of the 'old' order, whose demise was only a matter of time, the USSR became a society dominated by a political leadership possessing a single-minded determination to survive at all costs. Military strength was the chosen instrument of security; the economy was developed in such a manner as to provide the means. The sense of historic mission has now evaporated, but the structures remain. Encumbered by the inheritance of a hypertrophied defence industry, the Soviet Union is attempting to forge a new path of development, to return to the world community from which it excommunicated itself more than seventy years ago.

This policy turn is Gorbachev's singular achievement. In the words of the former prime minister, Valentin Pavlov, the need now is 'to get away from the cumbersome structure of a militarized economy, to a normal, people's economy'.[20] In short, demilitarization is an essential condition for de-utopianization. The return to a 'normal', civil path will be a long, difficult process, but one in which the defence industry itself could play a significant part. But it also has the potential to obstruct this path, to frustrate all efforts for reform, with consequences that could extend far beyond Soviet borders. As a fateful utopian experiment comes to an end, it is not only Soviet citizens who have a stake in the successful scaling down, conversion and reform of the military core of the exhausted command economy.

NOTES

Chapter 1

1 *Pravda*, 8 December 1988 and 19 January 1989.
2 *Pravda*, 8 June 1989; BBC, *Summary of World Broadcasts*, SU/0641 i, 16 December 1989.
3 *Krasnaya Zvezda*, 13 November 1990.
4 *Trud*, 21 December 1990.
5 Ibid.; and *Krasnaya Zvezda*, 13 December 1990.
6 BBC, *Summary of World Broadcasts*, SU/0960 C1/2, 3 January 1991, and SU/0966 C1/4, 10 January 1991.
7 *Krasnaya Zvezda*, 11 and 12 January 1991; *Izvestiya*, 12 January 1991; BBC, *Summary of World Broadcasts*, SU/0968 C1/3–5, 12 January 1991.
8 For example, 'Soviet MPs rain roubles on military', *The Guardian*, 12 January 1991. For a more detailed discussion of the scale of military expenditure cuts see the author's 'Military Cuts and Conversion in the Defense Industry', *Soviet Economy*, vol. 7, no. 2, April–June 1991, pp. 121–42.
9 BBC, *Summary of World Broadcasts*, SU/0918 A1/4, 10 November 1990.

Chapter 2

1 *Pervaya sessiya Verkhovnogo Soveta SSSR. Stenograficheskii otchet*, Moscow, 1989, Part V, p. 24.
2 Ibid., p. 23.
3 *Flight International*, 9 September 1989, p. 26.

Notes

4   *Leningradskaya Pravda*, 31 August 1990.
5   Novosti Press Agency, Briefing Paper for the Conversion–90 Exhibition, Munich, 1990, p. 5.
6   *Planovoe Khozyaistvo*, 1990, no. 7, p. 4.
7   *Who's Who in the Soviet Government*, Novosti, Moscow, 1990, p. 127.
8   See J. Cooper, 'Military Cuts and Conversion in the Defense Industry', pp. 121–42.
9   International Labour Office (ILO), Disarmament and Employment Programme, *Working Paper*, no. 16, March 1990, p. 12.
10 *Komsomol'skaya Pravda*, 29 November 1990 (citing a report of the Moscow-based International Fund for Conversion); *The Economy of the USSR – A study undertaken in response to a report of the Houston Summit. Summary and Recommendations*, International Monetary Fund (IMF), etc., 1990, p. 46. No sources or definitions are provided.
11 A Soviet author has stated that 14.4 million people are employed in the military-industrial complex (V. Pervyshin, *Ogonek*, 1991, no. 24, p. 8). It is not clear what credence can be given to this figure, since other data presented by the same author are of doubtful reliability.
12 A. F. Sidorov, *Sovershenstvovanie khozracheta v nauchno-proizvodstvennom ob"edinenii*, Moscow, 1985, p. 5. Note: the ministry then had 51 PO and 19 NPO, giving a total of 434 enterprises (calculated from Sidorov, *Sovershenshtvovanie khozracheta*, p. 36).
13 *Ekonomika i Zhizn'*, 1990, no. 29, p. 3.
14 *Pravda*, 30 July 1990.
15 Elsewhere, Smyslov has claimed that conversion is to be undertaken at more than 400 defence enterprises, 40 per cent of the total. This could simply be a misprint, or, alternatively, may involve a different definition of an enterprise engaged in military production (*Soviet News*, no. 6157, 14 March 1990, p. 90).
16 A. Kortunov of the USA Institute of the USSR Academy of Sciences, BBC, *Summary of World Broadcasts*, SU/0932 A1/2, 27 November 1990.
17 See *Soviet Economy*, vol. 7, no. 2, pp. 135–7.
18 *Izvestiya*, 14 January 1991.
19 *Izvestiya*, 21 May 1991.
20 It is notable that the State Committee for Statistics, Goskomstat, has no direct access to detailed statistical data on military R&D: the Ministry of Finance simply provides it with an aggregate total expenditure figure (*Voprosy Istorii Estestvoznaniya i Tekhnika*, 1990, no. 4, p. 124).
21 See J. M. Cooper, 'The Elite of the Defence Industry Complex' in D. Lane (ed.), *Elites and Political Power in the USSR*, Edward Elgar, Aldershot,

1988, pp. 174–87.

22 Ibid.

23 *Argumenty i Fakty*, 1989, no. 33, p. 2.

24 *Pravda*, 24 January 1991 (the author, I. Mosin, is described as a special correspondent of the paper).

Chapter 3

1 This database is being prepared for eventual publication. Since the statistical analysis presented here was undertaken, the number of establishments covered has expanded to more than one thousand.

2 The findings presented here are based on a larger database than that employed in the author's earlier work: ILO, Development and Employment Programme, *Working Paper*, no. 10, December 1988 ('The Soviet defence industry and conversion: the regional dimension').

3 I am grateful to Dr Michael Bradshaw of the School of Geography, University of Birmingham, for providing assistance in undertaking this regional analysis, and for preparing the map.

4 Many republics, former autonomous republics (ASSR) and cities have been renamed during the past two to three years. In such cases both new and old names are presented to avoid confusion.

5 *Poisk*, 1990, no. 50, p. 8.

6 Calculated from *Pravda*, 11 Janaury 1991. This source reveals that the Ministry of Defence permanently occupies 42 million hectares of territory, 2 per cent of the USSR total. Thus the Kazakh test sites account for more than 40 per cent of the total.

7 *Moskovskaya Pravda*, 24 October 1989.

8 *Nedelya*, 1990, no. 43, p. 3.

9 *Trud*, 22 November 1989.

10 *Leningradskaya Pravda*, 31 August 1990.

11 *The Economist*, 15 December 1990, p. 23; *Radikal* (Leningrad), 1990, no. 3, p. 2.

12 BBC, *Summary of World Broadcasts*, SU/0922 B/13, 15 November 1990 (Kovrov); *The Financial Times*, 20 November 1990; ITN, Channel Four News, 28 May 1991.

13 *Pravda*, 22 January 1991; *Krasnaya Zvezda*, 30 April 1991. See also J. Tedstrom, 'Industrial Conversion at the Local Level', RL/RFE, *Report on the USSR*, vol. 3, no. 25, 21 June 1991, pp. 19–23.

14 *Pravitel' stvennyi Vestnik*, 1990, no. 49, p. 3. Note that both are now self-proclaimed republics: Mariiel and Tatarstan respectively.

Notes

15 *Krasnaya Zvezda*, 19 October 1990. The 'Mayak' works was the location of the major nuclear waste accident of 1957 described by Zhores Medvedev in his book, *Nuclear Disaster in the Urals*, Angus & Robertson, London, 1979.

16 Information supplied by David Holloway, Stanford University.

17 *Trud*, 28 November 1990; *Krasnaya Zvezda*, 25 November 1990.

18 *Sotsialisticheskaya Industriya*, 9 August 1989; *Nedelya*, 1990, no. 26, p. 4; *Komsomol'skaya Pravda*, 22 November 1990; *Pravda*, 13 November 1989; *Trud*, 25 January 1991.

19 *Rabochaya Tribuna*, 11 January 1991.

20 *Izvestiya*, 3 May and 28 December 1990, 24 January 1991; *Pravda*, 23 August 1990.

21 *Izvestiya*, 12 April 1991.

22 *Komsomol'skaya Pravda*, 31 August 1989 and 25 November 1990; *Sotsialisticheskaya Industriya*, 9 August 1989; *Krasnaya Zvezda*, 19 October 1990.

23 *Argumenty i Fakty*, 1991, no. 1, p. 5.

24 *Trud*, 25 January 1991.

25 It is worth noting that the RBMK reactor of the Chernobyl power station was designed by the same team responsible for most of the reactors developed for the production of plutonium for nuclear weapons, including the very first plutonium reactor of 1948 at Chelyabinsk–40. The organization concerned, the Moscow Research and Design Institute of Power Equipment – for many years under Academician Nikolai Dollezhal', the chief designer of the RBMK – worked in conditions of the strictest secrecy.

26 *Rabochaya Tribuna*, 16 September 1990. Six people were killed.

27 *Komsomol'skaya Pravda*, 10 October 1990; *Rabochaya Tribuna*, 17 October 1990. A demand that this pollution be cleaned up featured in a list of grievances of workers of the town, who threatened strike action if nothing was done.

28 *Pravda*, 25 April 1990; *Trud*, 2 June 1990; *Krasnaya Zvezda*, 5 December 1990; *Sovetskaya Rossiya*, 2 November 1990.

29 A report of the Biisk factory explosion observed that this 'regime' works was so secret that not only were journalists barred from access after the accident, but even workers of the KGB and the militia! (*Rabochaya Tribuna*, 15 November 1990.)

30 *Izvestiya*, 25 November 1990.

31 *Izvestiya*, 26 January 1991.

Chapter 4

1 For a discussion of the political background, see the author's 'The Defense Industry and Civil-Military Relations' in T. J. Colton and T. Gustafson (eds.), *Soldiers and the Soviet State*, Princeton University Press, Princeton NJ, 1990, pp. 166–76.

2 See the author's 'The Civilian Production of the Soviet Defence Industry' in R. Amann and J. Cooper (eds.), *Technical Progress and Soviet Economic Development*, Blackwell, Oxford, 1986, pp. 31–50.

3 *Pravda*, 17 October 1987 and 9 July 1990.

4 Enterprises: *Ekonomika i Organizatsiya Promyshlennogo Proizvodstva*, 1990, no. 5, p. 157; labour: *Sotsialistichesii Trud*, 1988, no. 5, inside front cover; output: estimated from *Planovoe Khozyaistvo*, 1986, no. 3, p. 88, and S. I. Mozokhin and E. N. Tatarintsev, *Regional'naya organizatsiya mashinostroitel'nogo proizvodstva*, Moscow, 1984, p. 8; profit: *Ekonomicheskaya Gazeta*, 1988, no. 11, p. 20.

5 *Pravitel'stvennyi Vestnik*, 1989, no. 4, p. 2.

6 *Sel'skaya Zhizn'*, 21 February 1990.

7 *Ekonomika i·Organizatsiya Promyshlennogo Proizvodstva*, 1990, no. 5, p. 157.

8 See J. Cooper, 'Technology Transfers between Military and Civilian Ministries' in US Congress, Joint Economic Committee, *Gorbachev's Economic Plans*, Washington DC, 1987, vol. 1, pp. 388–404.

9 See, for example, *Trud*, 4 June 1989; *Moskovskaya Pravda*, 19 February 1989; *Vechernyaya Moskva*, 20 July 1989; and *Vestnik Mashinostroeniya*, 1990, no. 5.

10 *Pravitel'stvennyi Vestnik*, 1989, no. 17, p. 7.

11 *Izvestiya*, 28 February 1990.

12 *Pravda*, 1 December 1989.

13 See G. Khromov, 'Conversion from military to civilian production: the Votkinsk plant' in L. Paukert and P. Richards (eds.), *Defence expenditure, industrial conversion and local employment*, ILO, Geneva, 1991, pp. 179–88.

14 From the outset the most articulate critics of the traditional approach were Aleksei Izyumov of the Academy's USA Institute (see, e.g., *Novoe Vremya*, 1988, no. 30, pp. 21-2 and *Literaturnaya Gazeta*, 1989, no. 28, p. 11) and Aleksei Kireev, an economist attached to the International department of the Party Central Committee (e.g., *Novoe Vremya*, 1989, no. 4, pp. 14–7; and *Trud*, 5 May 1989).

15 See *Poisk*, 1990, no. 10, p. 4.

16 *Pravda*, 15 February 1990.

Notes

17 *Pravda*, 29 September 1990.

18 *Voprosy Ekonomiki*, 1991, no. 2, pp. 4–7 and 32.

19 *Pravda*, 30 July 1990; Report of V. G. Kotov (Gosplan) to the United Nations Conference on Conversion, Moscow, August 1990, p. 4.

20 Report by V. I. Smyslov (Gosplan) at the UN Conference on Conversion, Moscow, August 1990, p. 7.

21 *Soviet Economy*, vol. 7, no. 2, April–June 1991, pp. 127–31.

22 *Kommersant*, 1990, no. 32, p. 3.

23 *Poisk*, 1990, no. 10, p. 4. Kotov's superior, Yu. A. Glybin, has also hinted that enterprises undergoing conversion will retain an R&D potential making possible a resumption of military production. (*Ekonomika i Organizatsiya Promyshlennogo Proizvodstva*, 1990, no. 5, p. 164.)

24 *Ekonomika i Zhizn'*, 1991, no. 36, p. 11; *Ekonomicheskie Nauki*, 1990, no. 8, p. 36.

25 *Voprosy Ekonomiki*, 1991, no. 2, p. 8; *Krasnaya Zvezda*, 20 April 1991.

26 *Soyuz*, 1991, no. 24 (June), p. 11.

27 *SShA*, 1990, no. 2, p. 18.

28 *Pravda*, 30 July 1990; *Kommersant*, 1990, no. 32, p. 3.

29 *Izvestiya TsK KPSS*, 1990, no. 8, p. 126.

30 *Pravitel'stvennyi Vestnik*, 1990, no. 37, p. 8.

31 *Moskovskaya Pravda*, 24 October 1989.

32 Examples include M. P. Simonov, head of the Sukhoi design bureau (*Soyuz*, 1990, no. 7, p. 14) and R. A. Belyakov of the MiG bureau (*Moskovskaya Pravda*, 8 December 1989).

33 Report by V. I. Smyslov to United Nations Conference on Conversion, Moscow, August 1990, p. 9; *Ekonomika i Zhizn'*, 1990, no. 36, p. 11.

34 *Izvestiya*, 18 June 1990; *Komsomol'skaya Pravda*, 20 June 1990.

35 *Krasnaya Zvezda*, 27 October 1990.

36 When asked at a meeting when a Law on Conversion would appear, Pavlov answered, 'I don't know … Why has a fetish been made of a piece of paper?' (*Vesti Dubny*, 11 June 1991.)

37 *Rabochaya Tribuna*, 31 July 1991.

38 *Sobranie postanovlenii pravitel'stva SSSR*, 1st section, 1990, no. 20, decree no. 102; *Trud*, 24 October 1990.

39 *Leningradskaya Pravda*, 24 November 1989.

40 *Rabochaya Tribuna*, 22 February 1991.

41 *Izvestiya*, 21 September 1990 and 22 January 1991; *Krasnaya Zvezda*, 26 December 1990.

42 *Izvestiya*, 1 April 1990.

43 The contents of this report have been summarized in articles by Yaremenko and his colleagues Evgenii Rogovskii and Aleksandr Ozhegov: *Ekonomika i Zhizn'*, 1990, no. 36, p. 11; *Ekonomicheskie Nauki*, 1990, no. 8, pp. 33–9; *Kommunist*, 1991, no. 1, pp. 54–64.
44 *Pravda*, 1 September 1990.
45 *Izvestiya*, 28 October 1990.
46 BBC, *Summary of World Broadcasts*, SU/1025 C1/3, 20 March 1990.
47 *Pravda*, 8 May 1991.
48 BBC, *Summary of World Broadcasts*, SU/1048 B/4, 17 April 1991.
49 See, for example, *Pravda*, 11 July 1991 (A. Kokoshin) and *Literaturnaya Rossiya*, 1991, no. 26, p. 5 (S. Kuznetsov).
50 *Izvestiya*, 18 April 1991.
51 *Rabochaya Tribuna*, 8 June 1991.
52 *Rabochaya Tribuna*, 31 July 1991.

Chapter 5

1 A. Isaev, 'Reforma i oboronnye otrasli', *Kommunist*, 1989, no. 5, pp. 24–30.
2 *Sotsialisticheskaya Industriya*, 19 August 1989.
3 *Pravda*, 20 September 1990; *Rabochaya Tribuna*, 28 September 1990.
4 *Kommersant*, 1991, no. 2, (7–14 February), p. 4.
5 BBC, *Summary of World Broadcasts*, SU/W0177 A/11, 3 May 1991; *Pravda*, 2 July 1991.
6 *Ekonomika i Zhizn'*, 1991, no. 30, p. 6.
7 *Pravitel'stvennyi Vestnik*, 1991, no. 16, p. 8; *Izvestiya*, 29 June 1991.
8 *Kommercheskii Vestnik*, 1991, no. 1, p. 26.
9 *Pravda*, 15 September 1990.
10 *Vesti Dubny*, 11 June 1991.
11 *Izvestiya*, 6 July 1991; *The Guardian*, 26 June 1991.
12 *Poisk*, 1991, no. 25, p. 3.
13 *Rabochaya Tribuna*, 7 June 1991.
14 *Rabochaya Tribuna*, 19 January 1991.
15 *Kommersant'*, 1991, no. 15 (8–15 April), p. 6.
16 *Kommersant'*, 1991, no. 26 (24 June–1 July), p. 5.
17 *Pravda*, 19 June 1991; *Izvestiya*, 4 July 1991.
18 BBC, *Summary of World Broadcasts*, SU/1108 i, 26 June 1991.
19 *Sel'skaya Zhizn'*, 7 October 1990 (I. S. Silaev).
20 BBC, *Summary of World Broadcasts*, SU/0941 B/3, 7 December 1990.

These rates were later revised to 32 per cent for enterprises of Russian subordination and 35 per cent for union enterprises (*Kommersant'*, 1991, no. 20, p. 5).

21 *Izvestiya*, 4 February 1991.

22 *Inzhenernaya Gazeta*, 1991, no. 84, July.

23 *Pravda*, 14 February 1991.

24 *Pravda Ukrainy*, 23 May 1991; *The Independent*, 28 May 1991.

25 *Pravda Ukrainy*, 11 June 1991; *Izvestiya*, 12 April 1991; BBC, *Summary of World Broadcasts*, SU/1124 B/12, 15 July 1991.

26 *Izvestiya*, 18 June 1991; BBC, *Summary of World Broadcasts*, SU/1092 B/12, 7 June 1991.

27 *Izvestiya*, 9 March 1991.

28 *Izvestiya*, 27 June 1991.

29 *Krasnaya Zvezda*, 18 October 1990.

30 See *Krasnaya Zvezda*, 28 June 1990.

31 *Krasnaya Zvezda*, 12 January 1990.

32 *Krasnaya Zvezda*, 15 September 1990.

33 *Pravitel'stvennyi Vestnik*, 1990, no. 48, Supplement, p. 8 (the draft programme for military reform).

34 *Pravitel'stvennyi Vestnik*, 1991, no. 2, p. 12.

35 *Pravda*, 14 October 1988.

36 *Krasnaya Zvezda*, 27 June 1991.

37 *Izvestiya*, 7 February 1990.

38 *Izvestiya*, 20 February 1990.

39 *Sovetskaya Rossiya*, 14 and 20 January, and 1 and 4 February, 1990.

40 *Komsomol'skaya Pravda*, 16 June 1990 and 17 January 1991; *Ogonek*, 1991, no. 5, pp. 30–32; *Izvestiya*, 28 March 1991.

41 *Komsomol'skaya Pravda*, 24 and 28 October 1990.

42 *Pravda*, 9 February 1991; *Sovetskaya Rossiya*, 1 March 1991.

43 *Transition to the Market*, Part 1, Moscow, August 1990, pp. 62, 106–13 and 151 (translation produced by the Cultural Initiative Foundation, Moscow).

44 *Pravda*, 6 September 1990.

45 *Moscow News*, 1991, no. 8, pp. 8–9 ('The Monster: a profile of the Soviet military-industrial complex' by A. Izyumov and A. Kortunov).

46 See 'Soviet arms industry bows to the inevitable', *The Guardian*, 22 July 199, for a revealing account of these developments in the military-industrial centre of Perm.

Chapter 6

1 See J. M. Cooper, 'The Defense Industry and Civil-Military Relations', p. 168.
2 *Pravda*, 10 October 1990.
3 *Pravda*, 26 April 1991.
4 From details of the membership of the Central Committee presented in *Izvestiya TsK KPSS*, 1990, nos 10, 11 and 12.
5 *Pravda*, 31 October 1990; *Krasnaya Zvezda*, 31 October 1990.
6 *Pravda*, 23 April 1990.
7 *Leningradskaya Pravda*, 22 and 24 April 1990; *Sovetskaya Rossiya*, 23 October 1990.
8 *Leningradskaya Pravda*, 22 August 1990.
9 *Leningradskaya Pravda*, 6 April 1990.
10 *Leningradskaya Pravda*, 1 August 1990.
11 *The Guardian*, 27 April 1991.
12 *The Independent*, 16 July 1991.
13 *Radikal*, 1991, no. 10.
14 *Glasnost'*, 1991, no. 17, p. 3; *Krasnaya Zvezda*, 31 May 1991.
15 *Pravda*, 6 September 1990 ('Status – "oboronke"').
16 *Leningradskaya Pravda*, 26 August 1989. The impact of the new law was especially onerous for fast growing electronics-related enterprises such as 'Svetlana'.
17 *Moskovskaya Pravda*, 21 October 1989 and 21 December 1989.
18 BBC, *Summary of World Broadcasts*, SU/W0155 A/10, 23 November 1990.
19 See interview with Tizyakov, entitled 'The market today – a catastrophe', in *Inzhenernaya Gazeta*, 1991, no. 73 (June).
20 *Pravda*, 11 November 1990.
21 *Moskovskaya Pravda*, 13 December 1990.
22 *Sovetskaya Rossiya*, 9 December 1990; *Pravitel'stvennyi Vestnik*, 1990, no. 50, p. 5.
23 *Pravitel'stvennyi Vestnik*, 1990, no. 50, supplement.
24 *Sovetskaya Rossiya*, 22 December 1990; see also P. Almquist, 'The Letter of the 53', *Russia and the World*, Issue 19 (1991), p. 7.
25 *Pravda*, 10 January 1991.
26 *Inzhenernaya Gazeta*, 11 February 1991. See also Elizabeth Teague, 'Soviet Employers' Organization Celebrates First Birthday', RL/RFE, *Report of the USSR*, vol. 3, no. 26, 26 June 1991, pp. 17–20.
27 *Ekonomika i Zhizn'*, 1991, no. 11, p. 6.

28 For Tizyakov's views see *Ekonomika i Zhizn'*, 1991, no. 25 (June), p. 9.

29 *Izvestiya*, 9 July 1991.

30 *Nash Sovremmenik*, 1990, no. 1, pp. 3–4; *Sovetskaya Rossiya*, 2 March 1990; *Sovetskii Voin*, 1989, no. 22, p. 77. The latter reveals that an embittered Nepobedimyi retired when he was challenged in an election for his post as director.

31 *Morskoi Sbornik*, 1990, no. 7, p. 6.

32 *Edinstvo*, 19–25 November 1990; BBC, *Summary of World Broadcasts*, SU/1126 B/4, 17 July 1991.

33 *Rabochaya Tribuna*, 23 February 1990. Yarovoi is also a member of the USSR Congress of People's Deputies. For his role in the attempted coup, he was dismissed from his post as factory director by the Estonian authorities (*Izvestiya*, 23 August 1991).

34 *Soyuz*, 1991, no. 2, p. 6.

35 *Baltiiskoe Vremya*, 21 August 1990.

36 *Sovetskaya Estoniya*, 17 January 1991.

37 BBC, *Summary of World Broadcasts*, SU/1127 B/9, 18 July 1991.

38 B. Yeltsin, *Against the Grain*, London, 1990, p. 201.

39 *Kommersant*, 1991, no. 12 (18–25 March), p. 11.

40 *Leningradskaya Pravda*, 12 June 1991. The overall RSFSR vote for Yeltsin was 57 per cent, and for Ryzhkov 17 per cent (*Izvestiya*, 20 June 1991).

41 *Kommersant*, 1991, no. 12 (18–25 March), p. 11.

42 *Vechernyaya Moskva*, 20 September 1990.

43 *Rabochaya Tribuna*, 16 April 1991.

44 'The Monster' was the title of a striking example of this genre, an article over the names of A. Izyumov and A. Kortunov in *Moscow News*, 1991, no. 8, pp. 8–9. Kortunov later publicly distanced himself from this article, claiming that the authors' views had been misrepresented by the weekly (*Krasnaya Zvezda*, 27 March 1991).

45 Yuri Afanasyev, 'The coming dictatorship', *The New York Review of Books*, 31 January 1991, p. 38.

46 V. Pervyshin, 'Razorenie', *Ogonek*, 1991, no. 24, p. 9.

47 *Izvestiya*, 15 May 1991.

48 *Sovetskaya Rossiya*, 23 July 1991.

49 *Nezavisimaya Gazeta*, 15 August 1991.

50 *Pravda*, 20 August 1991.

51 *Izvestiya*, 23 August 1991.

52 BBC, *Summary of World Broadcasts*, SU/1164 C2/9, 30 August 1991.

53 *Izvestiya*, 22 August 1991.

54 BBC, *Summary of World Broadcasts*, SU/1164 C2/11, 30 August 1991.

Notes

Protasov is also a member of the National Commission for the Promotion of Conversion.

Chapter 7

1 *Kommunist Vooruzhennykh Sil*, 1991, no. 2, p. 53.
2 In March 1990 Shabanov declared that 'we must retain our industry's potential for mobilization. To say that the military danger has completely disappeared would, I think, be quite simply incorrect and impermissible, and our industry must be prepared should the need arise, i.e., it must have the capacity for mobilization.' (BBC, *Summary of World Broadcasts*, SU/ 0703 C1/2, 3 March 1990.)
3 *Trud*, 21 December 1990.
4 Ibid.
5 *Glasnost'*, 1991, no. 6, p. 1.
6 *The Independent*, 2 March 1991.
7 *Komsomol'skaya Pravda*, 10 May 1990.
8 *Kommersant*, 1991, no. 2, (7–14 January); *Krasnaya Zvezda*, 25 January 1991. The exhibition was originally planned for May.
9 *Pravda*, 1 January 1990 and 18 September 1989.
10 *Pravda*, 1 October 1990.
11 *Izvestiya*, 21 June 1991.
12 *Delovoi Mir*, 26 July 1990.
13 *Pravda*, 22 January 1990 and 1 December 1989.
14 Moscow Narodny Bank, *Press Bulletin*, no. 1024, 19 July 1989, p. 6.
15 BBC, *Summary of World Broadcasts*, SU/W0167 A/9, 22 February 1991.
16 *Trud*, 18 June 1991; *Kommersant'*, 1991, no. 18, (29 April–6 May), p. 6.
17 *SUPAR Report*, no. 10, January 1991, p. 124 (issued by the University of Hawaii).
18 See Karpov's article in *Izvestiya* (27 July 1991) following the Group of Seven meeting with Gorbachev.
19 *Izvestiya*, 27 July 1991.
20 BBC, *Summary of World Broadcasts*, SU/1000 B/9, 19 February 1991.

DRAMATIS PERSONAE

AVDUESVSKII, Vsevolod S.: chairman of the National Commission for the Promotion of Conversion. A prominent scientist of the military-space industry. Academician of the USSR Academy of Sciences.

BAKLANOV, Oleg D.: former first deputy chairman of the USSR Defence Council; previously Communist Party Central Committee Secretary for defence matters, including conversion. A member of the State Committee for the State of Emergency, which led the unsuccessful coup attempt of August 1991. A Ukrainian, born 1932.

BELOUSOV, Boris M.: former Minister of the Defence Industry. A Russian, born 1934.

BELOUSOV, Igor S.: former chairman of the Military-Industrial Commission, replaced by Maslyukov at the end of 1990. A Russian, born 1928.

KOKSANOV, Igor V.: former Minister of the Shipbuilding Industry. A Russian, born 1928.

KONOVALOV, Vitalii F.: former Minister of Atomic Power and Industry. A Russian, born 1932.

KUDRYAVTSEV, Gennadii G.: former Minister of Communications. A Russian, born 1941.

MASLYUKOV, Yurii D.: former chairman of the Military-Industrial Commission, deputy prime minister of the USSR. Chairman of Gosplan 1988–90. A Russian, born 1937.

110

MIRONOV, Vyacheslav P.: Deputy Minister of Defence for Armaments, replaced V. M. Shabanov in late 1990. A Russian, born 1938.

SHABANOV, Vitalii M.: former Deputy Minister of Defence for Armaments. A Russian, born 1923.

SHAPOSHNIKOV, Evgenii I.: Minister of Defence, appointed after the failed coup of August 1991. Formerly Commander-in-Chief of the air force. A Russian, born 1942.

SHIMKO, Vladimir I.: former Minister of the Radio Industry. A Russian, born 1938.

SHISHKIN, Oleg N.: former Minister of General Machinebuilding. A Russian, born 1934.

SMYSLOV, Vladimir I.: first deputy chairman of the former Gosplan (from early 1991, Ministry for Economics and Forecasting), responsible for planning military production and conversion. A Russian, born 1928.

SYSTSOV, Apollon S.: former Minister of the Aviation Industry. A Russian, born 1929.

TIZYAKOV, Aleksandr I.: former president of the National Association of State Enterprises and general director of the Sverdlovsk NPO 'Zavod imeni Kalinina', a missile-producing plant of the aviation industry. A member of the State Committee for the State of Emergency, which led the unsuccessful coup attempt of August 1991. A Russian, born 1926.

VOL'SKII, Arkadii I.: president of the USSR Scientific and Industrial Union. Following the attempted coup of August 1991 appointed a member of the interim USSR Economic Committee, his responsibilities including oversight of the defence industry. A Russian, born 1932.

YAREMENKO, Yurii A.: director of the Insitute for National Economic Forecasting of the USSR Academy of Sciences. Led work on an alternative concept of conversion. A part-time adviser to Gorbachev.

YAZOV, Dmitrii T.: former Minister of Defence. A member of the State Committee for the State of Emergency, which led the unsuccessful coup attempt of August 1991. A Russian, born 1923.

The Council on Foreign Relations publishes authoritative and timely books on international affairs and American foreign policy. Designed for the interested citizen and specialist alike, the Council's rich assortment of studies covers topics ranging from economics to regional conflict. If you would like more information, please write:

Council on Foreign Relations Press
58 East 68th Street
New York, NY 10021
Telephone: (212) 734-0400
FAX: (212) 861-1789